First World War
and Army of Occupation
War Diary
France, Belgium and Germany

48 DIVISION
Divisional Troops
477 South Midland Field Company Royal Engineers
5 June 1915 - 31 October 1917

WO95/2751/3

The Naval & Military Press Ltd
www.nmarchive.com
Published in association with The National Archives

Published by

The Naval & Military Press Ltd

Unit 10 Ridgewood Industrial Park,

Uckfield, East Sussex,

TN22 5QE England

Tel: +44 (0) 1825 749494

www.naval-military-press.com

www.nmarchive.com

This diary has been reprinted in facsimile from the original. Any imperfections are inevitably reproduced and the quality may fall short of modern type and cartographic standards.

© **Crown Copyright**
Images reproduced by permission of The National Archives, London, England, 2015.

Contents

Document type	Place/Title	Date From	Date To
Heading	WO95/2751/3		
Heading	48th Division BEF 2-1st S.M. Fld Coy R.E Became 477th S.M. Fld Coy R.E. Jun 1915 Oct 1917		
Heading	48th Division 2/1st S.M. Field Coy R.E Vol I 5-30.6.15		
Heading	War Diary Of 2/1st South Midland Field Co. R.E. From June 5 1915 To June 30 1915 Volume 1		
War Diary	Hatfield Peverel	05/06/1915	06/06/1915
War Diary	Southampton	06/06/1915	06/06/1915
War Diary	Havre	07/06/1915	07/06/1915
War Diary	No.5 Rest Camp	08/06/1915	08/06/1915
War Diary	Havre	09/06/1915	09/06/1915
War Diary	Steenwercke	10/06/1915	10/06/1915
War Diary	Romarin	11/06/1915	26/06/1915
War Diary	Bailleul	27/06/1915	27/06/1915
War Diary	Vieux Berquin	28/06/1915	28/06/1915
War Diary	Robecq	29/06/1915	29/06/1915
War Diary	Raimbert	30/06/1915	30/06/1915
Heading	48th Division 2/1st S.M. Field Coy R.E Vol II 1-31-7-15		
War Diary	Raimbert	01/07/1915	04/07/1915
War Diary	Labourse	04/07/1915	12/07/1915
War Diary	Noeux Les Mines	12/07/1915	13/07/1915
War Diary	Labourse	13/07/1915	16/07/1915
War Diary	Raimbert	17/07/1915	19/07/1915
War Diary	Berquette	19/07/1915	19/07/1915
War Diary	Doullens	19/07/1915	19/07/1915
War Diary	Authie	19/07/1915	31/07/1915
Heading	48th Division 2/1st S.M. Field Coy R.E Vol III From 1-31.8.15		
Heading	War Diary Of 2/1st Field Company S.M.R.E (48th Div) From 1st August 1915 To 31st August 1915		
War Diary	Authie	01/08/1915	28/08/1915
Heading	48th Division 2/1st S.M. Field Coy R.E. Vol IV Sept 15		
Heading	War Diary Of 2/1 S.M. Field Company R.E. 48th Division From Sep 1 To Sep 30 1915 (Volume 4)		
War Diary	Authie	01/09/1915	09/09/1915
War Diary	Rossignol Farm	09/09/1915	14/09/1915
War Diary	Hebuterne	15/09/1915	20/09/1915
War Diary	Rossignol	21/09/1915	25/09/1915
War Diary	Rossignol Farm	26/09/1915	30/09/1915
Diagram etc	Diagram		
Map	Map		
Diagram etc	Diagram		
Heading	48th Division 2/1 S.M. Fd. Co. R.E. Oct 15 Vol V		
Heading	War Diary Of 2/1st S.M Field Company R.E From Oct 1 To Oct 31 1915 (Volume 5)		
War Diary	Rossignol Farm	01/10/1915	02/10/1915
War Diary	Hebuterne	03/10/1915	14/10/1915
War Diary	Rossignol	14/10/1915	30/10/1915
War Diary	Hebuterne	31/10/1915	31/10/1915

Miscellaneous	Extracts From Weekly States		
Heading	War Diary Of 2/1 S.M. Field Coy R.E 48th Div From Nov 1 To Nov. 30 1915 Volume 6		
War Diary	Hebuterne	01/11/1915	15/11/1915
War Diary	Rossignol Farm	15/11/1915	30/11/1915
Heading	48th Div 2/1st S.M Fd. Co. R.E Dec Vol VII		
War Diary	Rossignol Farm	01/12/1915	01/12/1915
War Diary	Hebuterne	02/12/1915	17/12/1915
War Diary	Rossignol Farm	18/12/1915	26/12/1915
Heading	War Diary Of 2/1 South Midland Field Co R.E 48th Division From Jan 1 To Jan 31 1916 (Volume 8)		
War Diary	Hebuterne	01/01/1916	12/01/1916
War Diary	Rossignol Farm	12/01/1916	24/01/1916
War Diary	Hebuterne	25/01/1916	31/01/1916
Miscellaneous	Extract From Weekly States		
Diagram etc	Diagram		
Heading	War Diary Of 2/1 S.M Field Company R.E From Feb 1 To Feb 29 1916 Volume 9		
War Diary	Hebuterne	01/02/1916	09/02/1916
War Diary	Rossignol	10/02/1916	13/02/1916
War Diary	Bienvillers Souastre	13/02/1916	28/02/1916
War Diary	Bienvillers	23/02/1916	29/02/1916
Heading	War Diary Of 2/1 South Midland Field Co. R.E (T) From 1st March 1916 To 31st March 1916 (Volume 10)		
War Diary	Souastre	01/03/1916	03/03/1916
War Diary	Colincamps	04/03/1916	31/03/1916
Heading	War Diary Of 2/1 South Midland Field Co R.E From April 1 To 30th 1916 (Volume 11)		
War Diary	Colincamps	02/04/1916	02/04/1916
War Diary	Sailly Au Bois	03/04/1916	22/04/1916
Diagram etc	Diagram		
Heading	War Diary Of 2/1 South Midland Field Company R.E. From May 1 To 31 1916 (Volume 12)		
War Diary	Sailly Au Bois	01/05/1916	03/05/1916
War Diary	Rossignol Farm	04/05/1916	04/05/1916
War Diary	Hem	05/05/1916	15/05/1916
War Diary	Rossignol Farm	16/05/1916	30/05/1916
War Diary	Sailly	30/05/1916	31/05/1916
Heading	War Diary Of 2/1 South Midland Field Co. R.E From 1st June 1916 To 30th June 1916 (Volume 13)		
War Diary	Sailly	01/06/1916	02/06/1916
War Diary	Hem	03/06/1916	11/06/1916
War Diary	Rossignol	12/06/1916	30/06/1916
War Diary	Rossignol Farm	01/07/1916	01/07/1916
War Diary	Mailly Maillet	02/07/1916	03/07/1916
War Diary	Rossignol	04/07/1916	05/07/1916
War Diary	Courcelles	06/07/1916	16/07/1916
War Diary	Aveluy	17/07/1916	29/07/1916
War Diary	Domqueur	31/07/1916	31/07/1916
Heading	48th Divisional Engineers 2/1st South Midland Field Company R.E. August 1916		
War Diary	Domqueur	03/08/1916	08/08/1916
War Diary	Longvillers	09/08/1916	09/08/1916
War Diary	Authieule	10/08/1916	10/08/1916
War Diary	Acheux	13/08/1916	13/08/1916
War Diary	Aveluy	15/08/1916	27/08/1916

War Diary	Mailly Maillet	28/08/1916	31/08/1916
Heading	48th Divisional Engineers 2/1st S.M. Field Coy Royal Engineer September 1916		
Heading	War Diary Of 2/1 South Midland Field Company R.E From 1-9-16 To 30-9-16 (Volume 16)		
War Diary	Mailly Maillet	05/09/1916	10/09/1916
War Diary	Bus	11/09/1916	11/09/1916
War Diary	Longvillette	13/09/1916	13/09/1916
War Diary	Hem	14/09/1916	18/09/1916
War Diary	Mezerolles	24/09/1916	24/09/1916
War Diary	Bernaville	29/09/1916	29/09/1916
Heading	War Diary Of 2/1st South Midland Field Co. R.E (T) From 1st Oct 1916 To 31st Oct 1916 (Volume 17)		
War Diary	Sus-St-Leger	01/10/1916	01/10/1916
War Diary	Halloy	03/10/1916	03/10/1916
War Diary	Grenas	04/10/1916	04/10/1916
War Diary	Souastre	05/10/1916	20/10/1916
War Diary	Warlincourt	24/10/1916	25/10/1916
War Diary	Bresle	26/10/1916	26/10/1916
War Diary	Mametz Wood	27/10/1916	31/10/1916
Miscellaneous	Extract From Weekly States		
Heading	War Diary Of 2/1st South Midland Field Company Royal Engineers From 1st Nov 1916 To 30th Nov 1916 (Volume 18)		
War Diary	Mametz Wood	03/11/1916	30/11/1916
Miscellaneous	Extract From Weekly States		
Heading	War Diary Of 2/1st South Midland Field Co. Royal Engineers From 1st Decr 1916 To 31st Dec 1916 (Volume 19)		
War Diary	Mametz Wood S.13.b 33	01/12/1916	30/12/1916
Miscellaneous	Extract From Weekly Returns		
Heading	War Diary Of 2/1st (South Midland) Field Company R.E From 1st January 1917 To 31st January 1917 Vol 20		
War Diary	Mametz Wood S 13 B 33	04/01/1917	27/01/1917
War Diary	Cerisey	30/01/1917	30/01/1917
Heading	War Diary Of 477 (South Midland) Field Coy. R.E From February 1st To February 28th 1917 Volume 21		
War Diary	Cerisey	01/02/1917	01/02/1917
War Diary	Frise	03/02/1917	14/02/1917
War Diary	Bois Vert	17/02/1917	28/02/1917
Miscellaneous	Extract From Weekly States		
Heading	War Diary Of 477th S.M. Field Co R.E. From 1st March 1917 To 31st March 1917 (Volume 22)		
War Diary	Boisvert	01/03/1917	18/03/1917
War Diary	Garden Farm 0.8.d.75	19/03/1917	19/03/1917
War Diary	Doingt	21/03/1917	27/03/1917
War Diary	Tincourt	28/03/1917	28/03/1917
War Diary	Hamel	29/03/1917	31/03/1917
Miscellaneous	Extract From Weekly States		
Heading	War Diary Of 477th South Midland Field Company Royal Engineers From 1st April 1917 To 30th April 1917 (Volume 23)		
War Diary	Tincourt	01/04/1917	18/04/1917
War Diary	Nr Rosel K4a. K4b	19/04/1917	23/04/1917
War Diary	Villers Faucon St Emilie & M Roisel	23/04/1917	26/04/1917

War Diary	Templeux La Fosse	26/04/1917	28/04/1917
War Diary	Viller Faucon St Emilie Nr Roisel	29/04/1917	30/04/1917
Miscellaneous	Extract From Weekly States		
Heading	War Diary Of 477th (S.M.) Field Co R.E From 1st May 1917 To 31st May 1917 (Volume 24)		
War Diary	Villers Faucon	01/05/1917	12/05/1917
War Diary	Peronne	15/05/1917	15/05/1917
War Diary	Combles	16/05/1917	16/05/1917
War Diary	Lebucquiere	17/05/1917	31/05/1917
Miscellaneous	Extracts From Weekly States		
Heading	War Diary Of 477th (S.M) Field Company Royal Engineers From 1st June 1917 To 30th June 1917 (Volume 25)		
War Diary	Lebucquiere	01/06/1917	30/06/1917
Miscellaneous	Extracts From Weekly States		
Heading	War Diary 477 (S.M) Field Coy R.E Vol 26-(3 Sheets) From 1/7/17 To 31/7/17		
War Diary	Lebucquiere	01/07/1917	01/07/1917
War Diary	Bihucourt	02/07/1917	12/07/1917
War Diary	Poperinghe	12/07/1917	31/07/1917
War Diary	Camp H.4.C	31/07/1917	31/07/1917
Heading	War Diary Of 477th S.M Field Company R.E. From 1st August 1917 To 31st August 1917 (Volume 27)		
Diagram etc	Diagram		
War Diary	Camp H.4.C	01/08/1917	05/08/1917
War Diary	Canal Bank N Of Ypres	05/08/1917	29/08/1917
War Diary	Camp G6.a.57	31/08/1917	31/08/1917
Heading	War Diary Of 477th South Midland Field Coy Royal Engineers From 1st Sept 1917 To 30th Sep 1917 (Volume No. 28)		
War Diary	Camp G.6.a.57	01/09/1917	28/09/1917
War Diary	Pesel Hoek	30/09/1917	30/09/1917
Heading	War Diary Of 477th (S.M.) Field Co R.E (Volume 29)		
War Diary	East Canal Bank	01/10/1917	10/10/1917
War Diary	Brown Camp	15/10/1917	31/10/1917
Miscellaneous	Extract From Weekly States		
Heading	War Diary Of 477 S.M. Field Company R.E (Volume 30)		

woods/27511/3

48TH DIVISION

BEF

2-1ST S.M. FLD COY R.E.
BECAME:-
477TH S.M. FLD COY R.E.
JUN 1915 - ~~MAR 1919.~~ OCT 1917

TO ITALY

121/5802

BS/
DJW

48th Division

2/1st S.M. Field Coy: RE

Vol I — 5 — 30.6.15.
1
Nov. '19

4/11st

CONFIDENTIAL

WAR DIARY

of

2/1st SOUTH MIDLAND FIELD Co. R.E.

from June 5 1915 to June 30 1915

(Volume 1).

Army Form C. 2118.

vol 1 sheet 1.

WAR DIARY
or
INTELLIGENCE SUMMARY.
(Erase heading not required.)

Instructions regarding War Diaries and Intelligence Summaries are contained in F. S. Regs., Part II. and the Staff Manual respectively. Title pages will be prepared in manuscript.

Place	Date	Hour	Summary of Events and Information	Remarks and references to Appendices
	1915			
HATFIELD PEVEREL	June 5	7-45p.	Received orders for Company to proceed abroad	
"	6	6-35a.	First half of Company entrained at WITHAM.	
"	6	9-5a.	Second half of Company entrained at WITHAM.	
SOUTHAMPTON	6	6-0p.	Horses vehicles and 115 A.R. departed on S.S. BELLEROPHON	
			100 A.R. departed on S.S. QUEEN EMPRESS.	
HAVRE	7	4-30a	S.S. BELLEROPHON arrived	
"	7	5-0 a.	S.S. QUEEN EMPRESS arrived	
"	7	7-30 a	Disembarked & proceeded to Nos Rest Camp. 1 driver injured through horse falling.	
Nos Rest Camp.	8		Inspected by O.C. troops in Camp	
HAVRE	9	7-0p.	Entrained in heavy thunder storm, all wet through.	
STEENWERCKE	10	12 noon.	Detrained and proceeded by march route to billet ROMARIN.	
			Capt. E. BRIGGS appointed to company from 1/1st S.M. Fd. Co. R.E. also 2/Lt. J.B. WATLING from 1/1st S.M. Fd. Co R.E. & 2/Lt R.J. WATTS from 1/2nd S.M. Fd. Co. R.E. 2/Lt. G.T. HOLLINGSWORTH transferred to 1/1st S.M. Fd. Co. R.E. This completed the complement of officers to the Company. Joined 48th Division.	

Army Form C. 2118.

WAR DIARY
or
INTELLIGENCE SUMMARY.
(Erase heading not required)

Vol. 1 Sheet 2.

Place	Date	Hour	Summary of Events and Information	Remarks and references to Appendices
ROMARIN	1915 June 11		3 sections working with 7th Fd. Co. R.E. on supporting points in rear of front line in HUNTER'S AVENUE - PLUG STREET Wood. 1 section working on supporting point round IN DEN KRAAIENBERG Cabaret in rear of front line.	
	" 12 to " 16		2 sections with 7th Co. R.E. "do" "do". 1 section IN DEN KRAAIENBERG as above. 1 section working on supporting strong point in rear of 2nd line CHATEAU de la HUTTE.	
	" 17 to " 20		7th Co. R.E. left the 48th Division & this Company took over their work on the line working with 144th Inf. Bde. who were then in reserve. 1 section at CHATEAU de la HUTTE. 1 " Constructing dug-out for G.O.C. 48th div. 150± w. of VILLA ROOZENBERG west end of HILL 63. 1 section making track in straight line from Div. H.Q. MIEPPE to G.O.C. dug-out HILL 63. 1 section making and erecting huts in wood behind w. end of HILL 63.	

Army Form C. 2118.

WAR DIARY
or
INTELLIGENCE SUMMARY.
(Erase heading not required.)

Vol. 1 sheet 3.

Instructions regarding War Diaries and Intelligence Summaries are contained in F.S. Regs., Part II. and the Staff Manual respectively. Title pages will be prepared in manuscript.

Place	Date	Hour	Summary of Events and Information	Remarks and references to Appendices
	1915			
REMMAR IN	June 21st	6	Took over left sector of the 48th Div. line held by 144th Inf. Bde. Trenches 37 & 73.	
	" 23		1 section billeted at CHATEAU de la HUTTE stables converting the buildings into strong defensive post.	
			1 section working on 2nd line supporting points by day.	
			1 section " " front line " " night and communication trench	
			1 section " " "anti-gas" switch across East end of HILL 63.	
	" 24		2 sections working at CHATEAU stables.	
	" 25		Resting.	
	" 26	10/1.	Handed over to 1st & 3rd Companies CANADIAN ENGINEERS. and proceeded by march route to billets S.W. of BAILLEUL 11 miles. Marched with Brigade	
	~~27~~		Group C under orders of G.O.C. 144th Inf. Bde.	
BAILLEUL	" 27	9-38p.	Proceeded by march route to billets in vicinity of VIEUX BERQUIN. 3 miles.	
VIEUX BERQUIN	" 28	6-41.	" " " " " " ROBECQ. 10 miles	
ROBECQ.	" 29	6-37	" " " " " " RAIMBERT 2m. S. of BURBURE 9 miles	
RAIMBERT	" 30		Checking stores, cleaning up etc.	

Whiff Capt.

48th Division.

2/1st S.M. Field Coy: R.E.

Vol II

1-31-7-15

19/6250

Army Form C. 2118.

Sheet 1

WAR DIARY
or
INTELLIGENCE SUMMARY.
(Erase heading not required.)

Instructions regarding War Diaries and Intelligence Summaries are contained in F.S. Regs., Part II. and the Staff Manual respectively. Title pages will be prepared in manuscript.

Place	Date	Hour	Summary of Events and Information	Remarks and references to Appendices
RAMBERT	July 1 to July 3		In Corps reserve – general training – practising attack etc.	
"	July 4	7-20a	Received orders to move to LABOURSE to work there on second line defences under Major Wallen R.E. 4th Corps.	
"	"	1-30p	Left RAMBERT	
LABOURSE	"	7-0p	Reached LABOURSE – bivouaced in field for night as no billets available.	
"	" 6	to	Started work on 2nd line trenches, completing revetment, covering parapets with sods etc & generally finishing off parts completed.	
"	" 11			
"	" 12	11-0a	Established work on 210 x & fire trench to be sapheading.	
"			Trench 50 x & in front of second line trenches S.E. of SAILLY LABOURSE	
"		11-0a	Received orders to be ready to move at 2pm to NOEUX les MINES or other place to be notified.	
"		2-p	All ready to move off.	
"		8-57p	Orders received to move to NOEUX les MINES	
NOEUX les	"	9-10p	Arrived at NOEUX les MINES & bivouaced for night in bicyclefield.	
MINES	" 13	9.a	Warned that we should be ready to move at any moment.	

Army Form C. 2118.

Sheet 2.

WAR DIARY
or
INTELLIGENCE SUMMARY.
(Erase heading not required.)

Place	Date	Hour	Summary of Events and Information	Remarks and references to Appendices
NOEUX les MINES	1915 July 13	3-p	Orders received to move back to our old billets at LABOURSE.	
LABOURSE	"	4-55p	Move complete - back in same billets - period 2 day's work wanted.	
"	14	6-0a	Continued work on supporting line in rear of 2nd line E. of SAILLY LABOURSE with 2 reliefs of infantry from 145th Bde., each of 700 men	
"	15	7-0a	Work continued on same line again with 2 reliefs of 700 men from 145th Bde. 670' of fire trench completed dug out. Communication trenches & dug outs in rear traced out & partly dug.	
"	16	7-0a	Work continued with 2 reliefs of 700 men from 145th Bde. and 700 men from 143rd Inf. Bde.	
"	16	9-0p	Proceeded by march route to RAIMBERT via NOEUX les MINES - BRUAY - AUCHEL (12 miles) A very wet night, everyone wet through.	
RAIMBERT	17	2-0a	Arrived at RAIMBERT and billeted there	
"	18		Baths & cleaning up generally	
"	19	4-45a	Proceeded to BERGUETTE by march route (8 miles)	
BERGUETTE	19	7-51a	Arrived BERGUETTE station & proceeded to entrain, started at 8-5 a.m.	
"	19	9-15a	Entrainment complete (1hr 10 mins).	

Army Form C. 2118.

Sheet 3.

WAR DIARY
or
INTELLIGENCE SUMMARY.
(Erase heading not required.)

Place	Date	Hour	Summary of Events and Information	Remarks and references to Appendices
BERGUETTE	1915 July 19	10-50a	Train departed.	
DOULLENS	"	3-55p	Arrived at DOULLENS and proceeded to detrain.	
	"	5-15p	Detrainment completed (1 hr 15 mins). An unfortunate accident occurred by which a man of the K.R.B. was killed during the unloading of the G.S. Wagon (technical)	
	"	5-20p	Proceeded to AUTHIE by march route via AUTHIEULE - ORVILLE - THIEVRES (10 miles.)	
AUTHIE		8-50p	Arrived at AUTHIE and billeted.	
	" 20	9-0a	Cleaning up wagon park & horse lines which were in a filthy state.	
	" 21	7-30a	Camping arrangements & water supply for 144th Infy Bde and other troops stationed around AUTHIE	
			1 Section to MARIEUX to work for Camp Commandant 7th Corps	
	" 22	7-0a	Camping arrangements. Took over work from the French in the Bois du HAMEL etc. Wood cutting, huddles, fascines, pickets etc making. Sawing trunks into planks at COIGNEUX	
	" 23	7-30a	1 Section working on drinking water supply for 7th Corps.	
			1 Section at MARIEUX working for 7th Corps.	

Army Form C. 2118.

Sheet 4.

WAR DIARY
or
INTELLIGENCE SUMMARY.
(Erase heading not required.)

Place	Date	Hour	Summary of Events and Information	Remarks and references to Appendices
AUTHIE	July 23		2 Sections working in BOIS du WARNIMONT and Camping arrangements, washing places for men, horse troughs for watering horses etc.	
	24	7:30a	1 Section at MARIEUX	
			1 Section at COIGNEUX – drinking water supply.	
			2 Sections in BOIS du WARNIMONT + Camping arrangements generally. N.C.O. and 7 men to III Army HQ's at BEAUQUESNE for work there. Arranged for hire of portable engine + saw bench to cut up trees in place of the laborious method employed by the French of cutting by hand.	
	25		Church Parade – Cleaning arms + checking stores.	
	26	7:30a	1 Section at MARIEUX	
			1 Section at COIGNEUX – drinking water supply	
	27	5:30p 7:30a	2 Sections cutting wood – Bundle making etc in BOIS du WARNIMONT. Reinforcements of 1 O₂? Section to BEAUQUESNE to work at III Army HQ's Do	
	28	6:30a	1 Section Attached to 7th Corps for work under C.E. on 3rd line between COIGNEUX + BERTRANCOURT.	
			Employed 600 men from 144th Inf Bde in completing fire trench + digging	

WAR DIARY
or
INTELLIGENCE SUMMARY.
(Erase heading not required.)

Army Form C. 2118.

Sheet 5.

Place	Date	Hour	Summary of Events and Information	Remarks and references to Appendices
AUTHIE	July 28		Communication trenches on No 1 work.	
	29	7.30a	1 Section at MARIEUX, 1 Sec. at BEAUQUESNE & 1 at COIGNEUX on drinking water supply	
	30	7.0a	"do" "do" 800 men from 144th Inf. Bde working on 3rd line.	
	31	7.0	"do" "do" 400 men from 144th & 400 men from 143rd Inf. Bdes on 3rd line Drinking water supply at COIGNEUX Complete. 150 galls. per hour of pure drinking water available and secure from contamination. Working party of 700 men from 143rd. Inf. Bde on 3rd line digging communication trenches & shelters also erecting high wire entanglement. Section from BEAUQUESNE returned to AUTHIE 1 Section still at MARIEUX working for 7th Corps at their HQ's.	

48th Division

2/1st S.M. Field Coy R.E.

Vol III

From 1.31.5.15

CONFIDENTIAL.

WAR DIARY

of

2/1st FIELD COMPANY. S.M.R.E. (48th Div)

From 1st August 1915 to 31st August 1915.

VOLUME 3

Army Form C. 2118.

vol 3 sheet 1

WAR DIARY
or
INTELLIGENCE SUMMARY.
(Erase heading not required.)

Instructions regarding War Diaries and Intelligence Summaries are contained in F. S. Regs., Part II. and the Staff Manual respectively. Title pages will be prepared in manuscript.

Place	Date	Hour	Summary of Events and Information	Remarks and references to Appendices
AUTHIE	1915 Aug 1 to Aug 9		3 sections working on 3rd line defences for 7th Corps, 600 infantry from brigade in reserve (46th Div) employed daily on Nos 1, 2 & 3 works, digging fire trenches, retelling and communication trenches, erecting entanglements and revetting fire trenches etc.	
	.10		1 Section deployed at HQ's 7th Corps MARIEUX on RE. service generally. 5 reinforcements (all sappers) joined	
			1 section moved to BUS du MAISNIMONT to superintend felling of trees, wood cutting, bundle & fascine making etc. 1 Section at 7th Corps HQ's. 2 Sections working on 2nd line defences for 7th Corps as above	
	-11		1 Section in BUS du MAISNIMONT work as above	
	-16		1 Section at 7th Corps HQ's	
			2 sections working on 3rd line defences, asking information of trenches etc.	
	-17		Major E. Hopps returned from Ecus (absence to England) (Aug 4 – 11)	
	-16	6pm	1 section returned to AUTHIE from 7th Corps HQ's MARIEUX	
	-17		2 sections working in BUS du MAISNIMONT as above	

Army Form C. 2118.

Vol 3 Sheet 2.

WAR DIARY
or
INTELLIGENCE SUMMARY.
(Erase heading not required.)

Instructions regarding War Diaries and Intelligence Summaries are contained in F. S. Regs., Part II. and the Staff Manual respectively. Title pages will be prepared in manuscript.

Place	Date	Hour	Summary of Events and Information	Remarks and references to Appendices
AUTHIE	1915 Aug 17	6	2 section working on 3rd line as above	
	Aug 22		2 sections " " as BOYS on MORNI MONT as above	
	Aug 21		Lt Matley proceeded on leave to England (Aug 21-28).	
	" 23		2 sections working in BOYS du MORNI MONT as above	
			Remainder of Company inspection of R.E. Stn, checking tools & cleaning up generally	
	" 24	6	2 section working in BOYS du MORNI MONT as above	
	" 31		2 sections working on 3rd line as above	
			Extract from weekly state	
			with unit Sept Serv Patty mounted &c	
			5 Offs 204 O.R. 6 nil nil (Reinforcements received).	
	" 7		5 " 207 " 10 nil	
	" 14		5 " 210 " 7 nil	
	" 21		5 " 209 " 8 nil	
	" 28			
			Plans "A" & "B" attached	
			A. Small scale plan showing situation of the works on 3rd line and state on Aug 31st	
			B. Larger scale plan showing details of No 2 work. Shipp Major.	

1577 Wt.W10791/1773 500,000 1/15 D. D. & L. A.D.S.S./Forms/C. 2118.

121/7100

48th Division

2/1st S.M. Field Cy RE

Vol IV

Sept. 15

CONFIDENTIAL.

War Diary

— of —

2/1 S. M. Field Company R.E.

48th Division

from Sep. 1 to Sep 30
1915

(Volume 4.)

Army Form C. 2118
Vol 4 Sheet 1.

WAR DIARY
or
INTELLIGENCE SUMMARY.
(Erase heading not required.)

Instructions regarding War Diaries and Intelligence Summaries are contained in F.S. Regs., Part II. and the Staff Manual respectively. Title pages will be prepared in manuscript.

Place	Date	Hour	Summary of Events and Information	Remarks and references to Appendices
AUTHIE	1915 Sep.1 to		2 sections working on 3rd line for 7th Corps.	
	Sep.8		2 sections working in BOIS du HAUT MONT felling trees etc.	
	Sep.9	10-0a	The Company, less No 3 section bivouaced in the BOIS du HAUT MONT, moved to new billets at ROSSIGNOL farm N. of COIGNEUX (Ref France sheet 12 1/80,000.)	
ROSSIGNOL farm	Sep.9 to		Work continued on 3rd line for 7th Corps & also in BOIS du HAUT MONT.	
	Sep.12			
	Sep.12		Drinking water supply, to supplement COIGNEUX supply, arranged for at COUIN and some watering troughs erected on R. AUTHIE at St LEGER L-s-AUTHIE.	
	Sep.13		1 section working on Corps line	
	"		1 section " in BOIS du HAUT MONT	
	"	6-0p.	1 section moved to HEBUTERNE to relieve section of 1st Sn Dvl Co. working on front line	
	"		1 section resting.	
	Sep.14	9-0a	1 section moved to SAILLY-au-BOIS to relieve section of 1st Sn H. Co.	
		6-0p.	2 sections moved to HEBUTERNE to relieve two sections of 1st Sn. Dvl Co.	
			H.Q. remains of Company remains at ROSSIGNOL farm	

Army Form C. 2118
Vol 4 sheet 2.

WAR DIARY
or
INTELLIGENCE SUMMARY.
(Erase heading not required.)

Instructions regarding War Diaries and Intelligence Summaries are contained in F. S. Regs., Part II and the Staff Manual respectively. Title pages will be prepared in manuscript.

Place	Date	Hour	Summary of Events and Information	Remarks and references to Appendices
HEBUTERNE	Sep. 18		3 Section at HEBUTERNE working on front line & HEBUTE RIVE inner defences	
	Sep. 19		1 section at SAILLY working on SAILLY defence line	
	Sep. 20		1 section returned to ROSSIGNOL farm for work on Corps line	
ROSSIGNOL	Sep. 21		2 sections returned to ROSSIGNOL farm for work on Corps line. 1 section to BOIS du WARENIMONT for wood cutting	
	" 22		2 sections working on Corps line with Hqs. working party of 600. 1 section wood cutting &c. in BOIS du WARENIMONT	
	" 23		1 section improving billet at ROSSIGNOT farm and arranging water supply at COUIN	
	" 24		3 sections loading pontoons, hauling tool carts &c. Collecting RE stores and materials at central stores at SAILLY & ROSSIGNOL farm. 1 section in BOIS du WARENIMONT cutting & sawing timber, preparing bridges &c. for expected advance.	
	" 25		1 section from BOIS du WARENIMONT returned to ROSSIGNOL farm. The Company practising pontooning & bridging	

Army Form C. 2118.

vol 4 sheet 3

WAR DIARY
or
INTELLIGENCE SUMMARY.

(Erase heading not required.)

Instructions regarding War Diaries and Intelligence Summaries are contained in F. S. Regs., Part II. and the Staff Manual respectively. Title pages will be prepared in manuscript.

Place	Date	Hour	Summary of Events and Information	Remarks and references to Appendices
ROSSIGNOL farm	Sept 26 to 28		The company engaged in practising pontooning, trestle & spar bridging and physical training	
	29		Work resumed on Capo line, 1 section superintending party up to from	
	30.		3rd bat Buffs; no infantry available	
			Reminder of company as on Sep. 26	
			Extracts from weekly states	
			With unit / Sick with unit / Killed wounded etc	
			O/S BOR		
Sept 4			5 204 1 nil unhospitalised
" 11			5 204 nil nil
" 18			5 205 2 nil 1 returned from hospital
" 25			5 206 nil nil 1 " " "

Briggs
Major

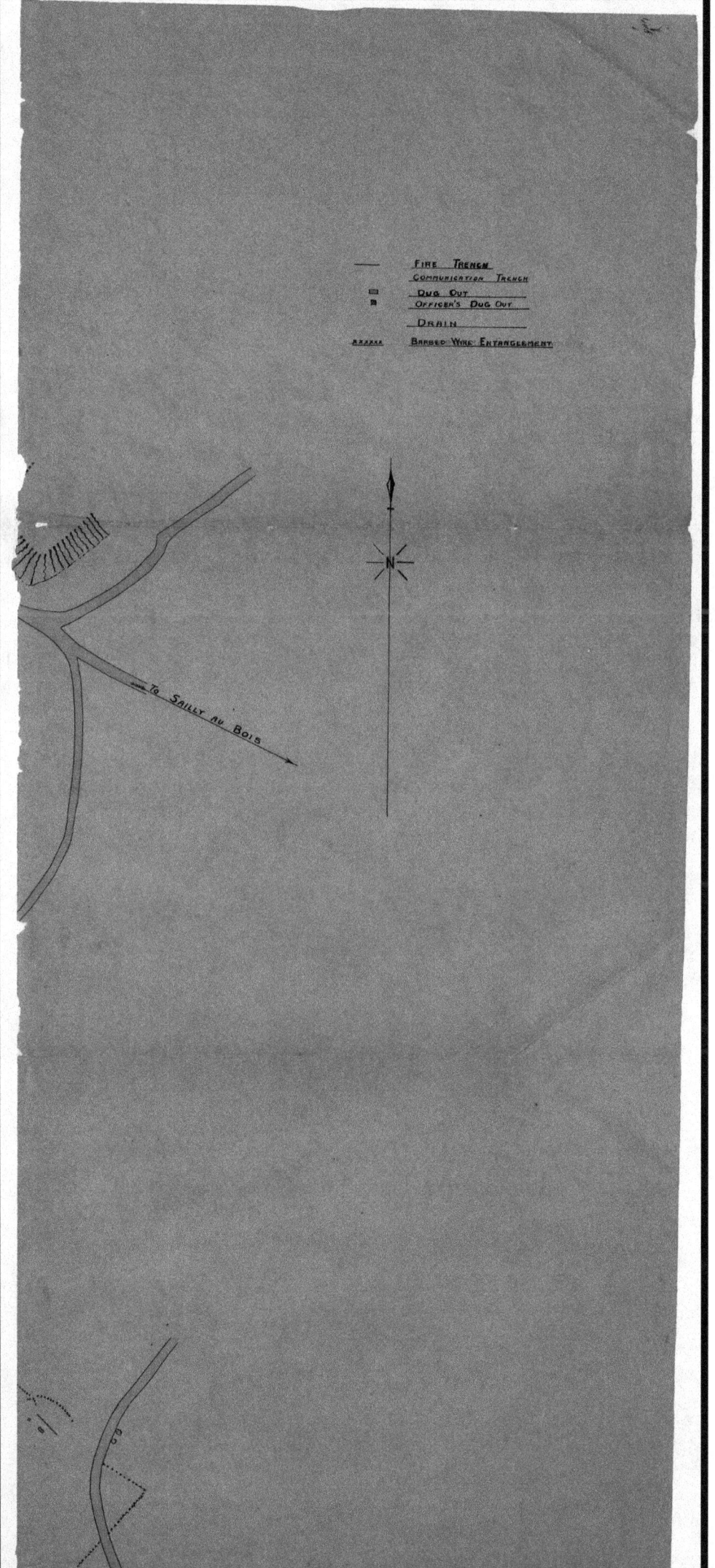

A

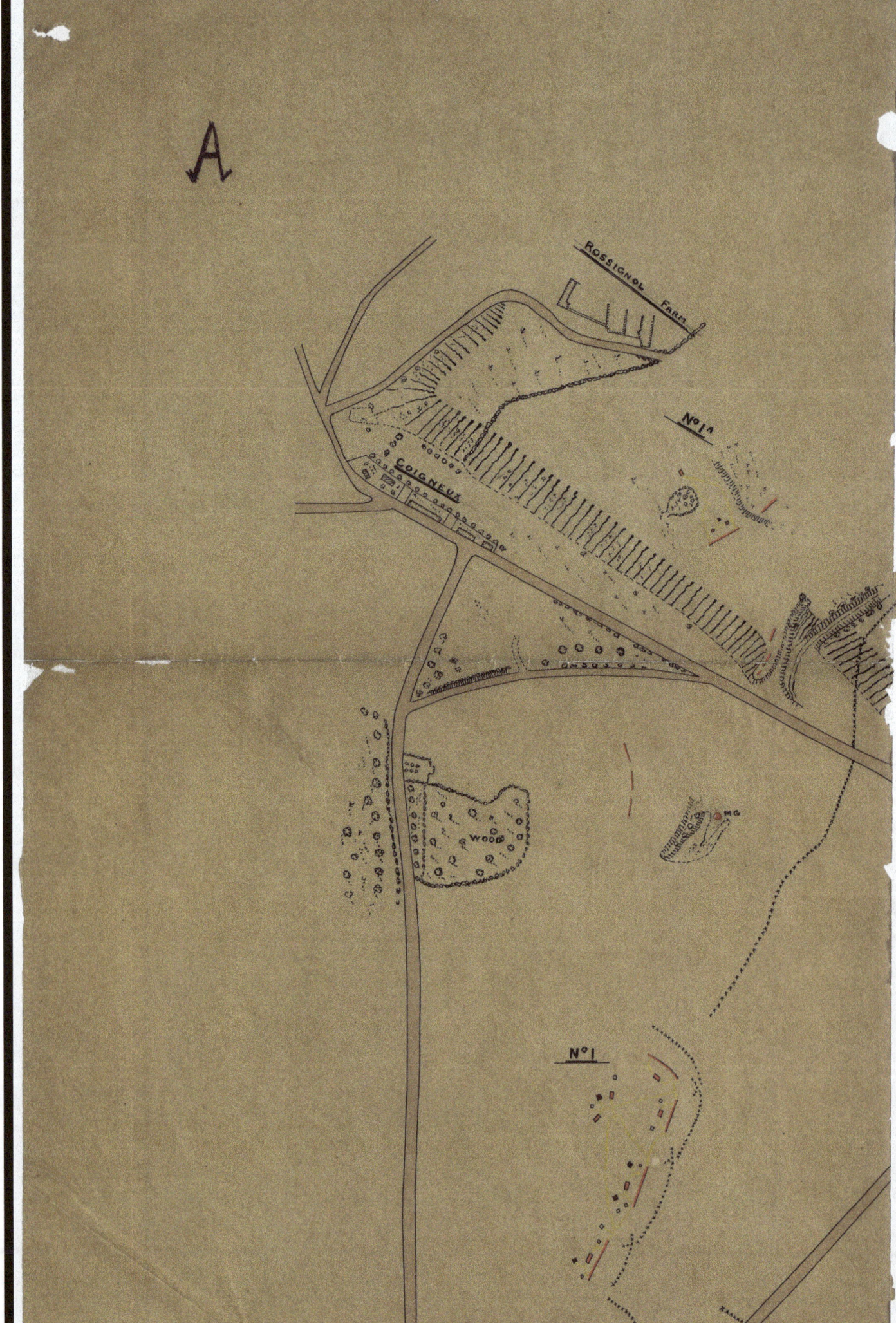

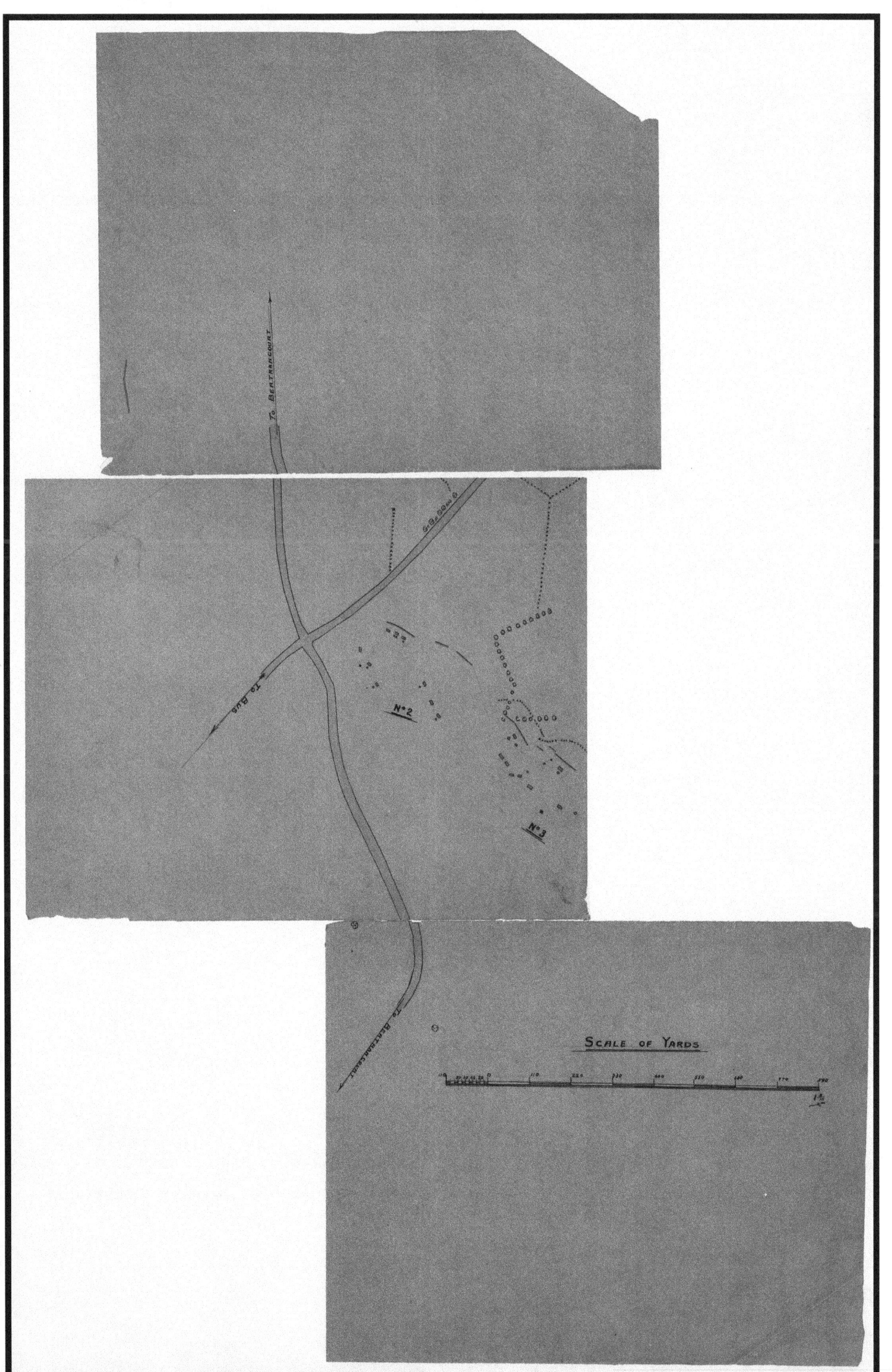

B

No 2

Traverse and Fire Trench
Communication Trench
Drain

Observation Post

Dug Out — Latrine
Dug Out — Latrine
Dug Out — Latrine

120

Dug Out
Dug Out — Latrine
Dug Out — Officer's Dug Out

Dug Out — Latrine
Kitchen — Latrine
Dug Out

Scale 1/1250 of/foot

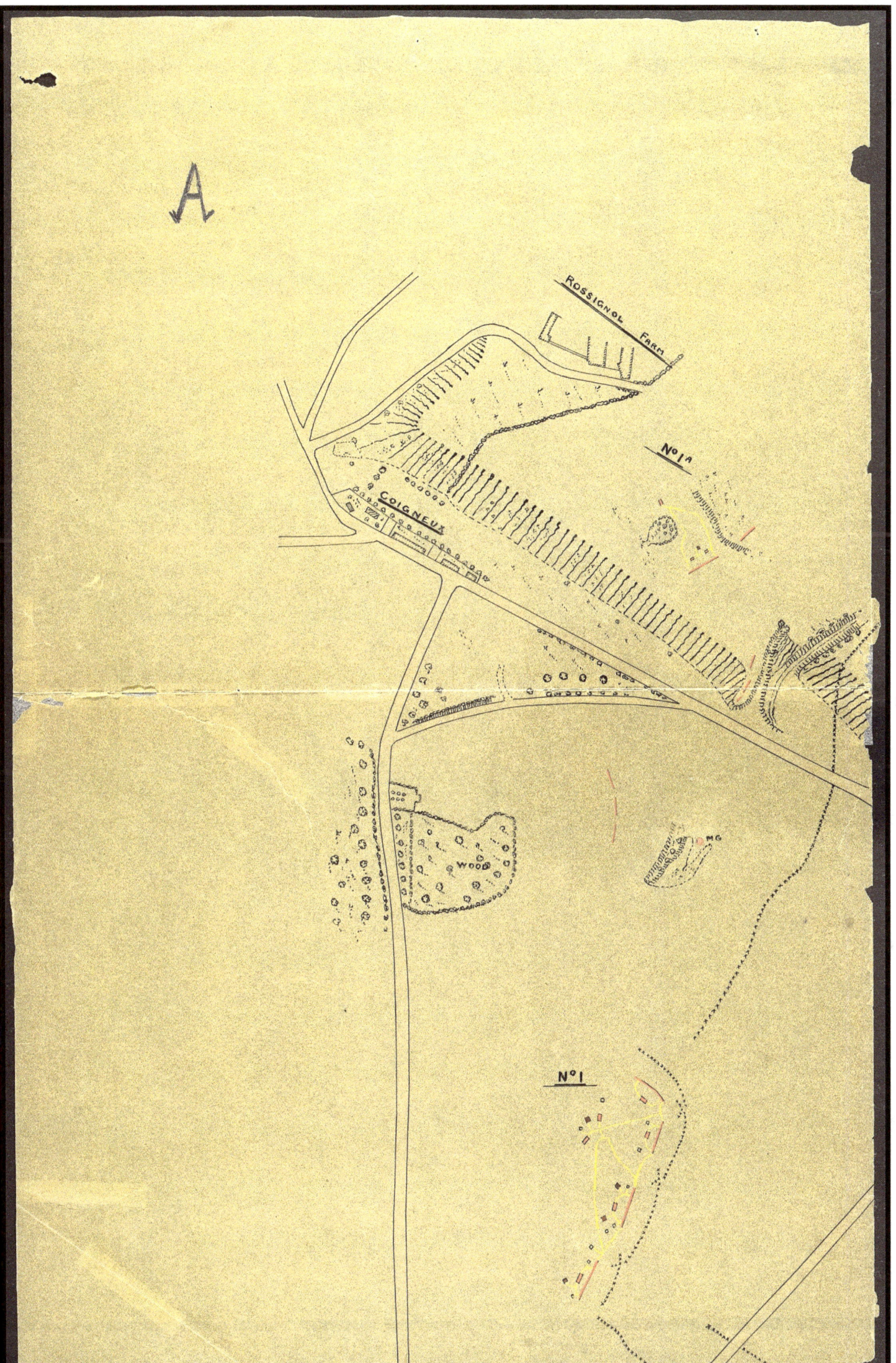

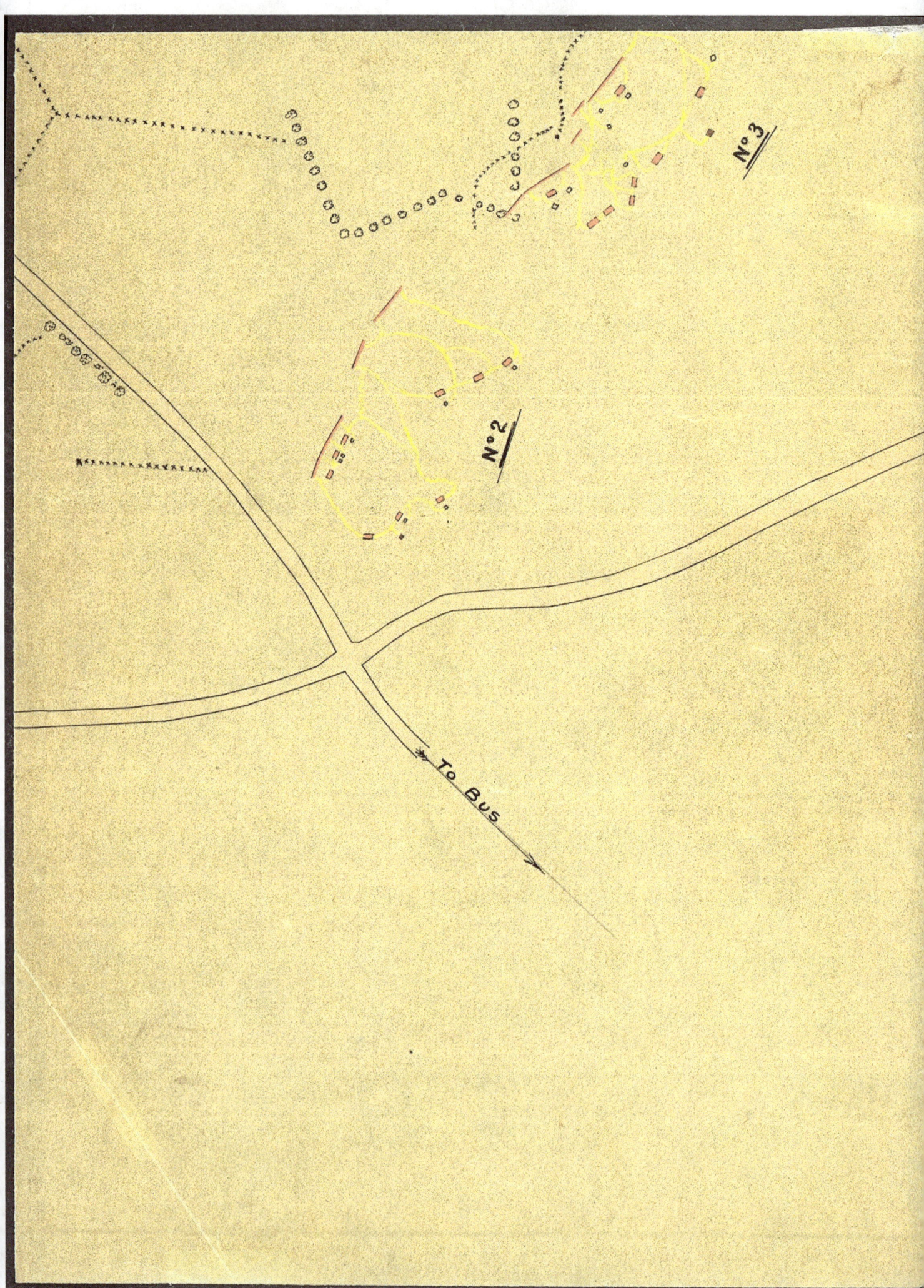

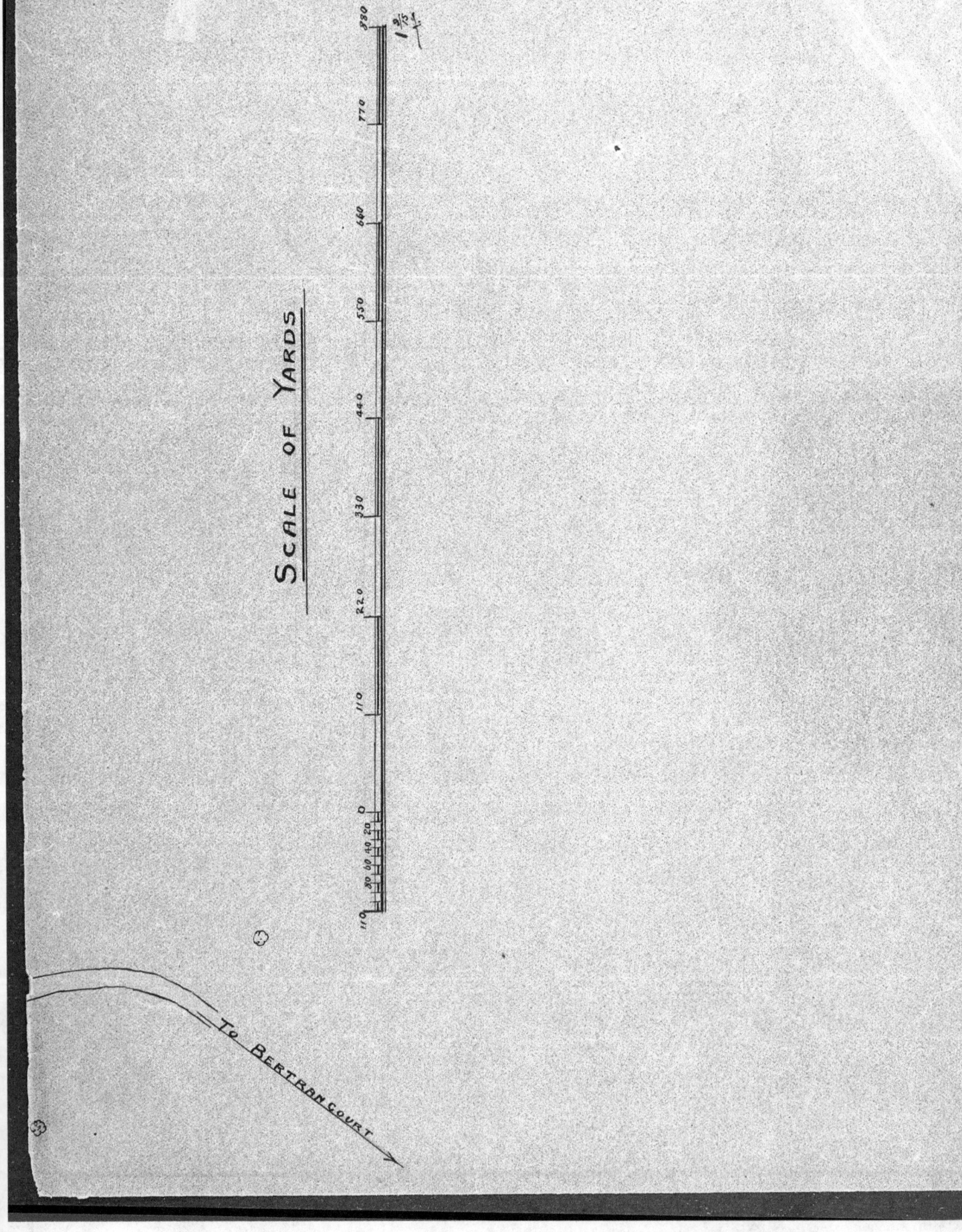

B

Nº 2

TRAVERSE AND FIRE TRENCH
COMMUNICATION TRENCH
DRAIN

㊱

㉔ OBSERVATION POST

⑥⓪ DUG OUT / LATRINE
KITCHEN / LATRINE

DUG OUT / LATRINE
OFFICERS DUG OUT
DUG OUT

DUG OUT / LATRINE
DUG OUT / LATRINE
DUG OUT / LATRINE

120

Scale 1/1250 offset

121/7470

48th Division

2/1 S.M. 2D Co. RE.

Oct '15

Vol II

CONFIDENTIAL.

WAR DIARY

— of —

2/1ˢᵗ S.M. FIELD COMPANY. R.E.

From Oct 1 to Oct 31 1915

(Volume 5.) 3 sheets.

Army Form C. 2118

vol 5 sheet 1

WAR DIARY
or
INTELLIGENCE SUMMARY.
(Erase heading not required.)

Place	Date	Hour	Summary of Events and Information	Remarks and references to Appendices
ROSSIGNOL farm	1915 Oct 1	8.0 a	Work continued on 7th Corps line	
		4 p	1 Section to HEBUTERNE + 1 Section to SAILLY.	
	2	4 p	2 Sections to HEBUTERNE.	
HEBUTERNE	Oct 3 to 10 m		2 Sections on day work. Work consisted of making dugouts, improving fire trenches & communication, laying pipes for water supply to front line trenches and R.E. services generally.	
	Oct 4		Reinforcements 1 officer 2nd Lt. Grandage and 1 driver reported on joining. 2nd Lt. L. Knipe to Divisional Rest Station suffering from shock caused by fall from horse, returned to duty on Oct 11th.	
	" 5			
	" 7		No. 1578 Sapper Bewbury N.F. wounded in two places while wiring in front of battalion reserve line.	
	Oct 13		1 Section from HEBUTERNE returned to ROSSIGNOL & ROSSIGNOL + 1 Section from SAILLY	
	" 14	5 am	Alarm of fire in HEBUTERNE. Two horses on fire. Fire put out by No 2 section with the aid of Lot-pumps, considerable damage was saved by their prompt action.	
	" 14	5 pm	Remaining 2 Sections from HEBUTERNE to ROSSIGNOL. Relieved at HEBUTERNE by 1st Sn. 2nd G. R.E.	

Army Form C. 21...

Vol 5 Sheet 2.

WAR DIARY
or
INTELLIGENCE SUMMARY.
(Erase heading not required.)

Place	Date	Hour	Summary of Events and Information	Remarks and references to Appendices
ROSSIGNOL	1915 Oct 14		Reinforcement of 2 sappers + 1 driver reported for duty.	
	Oct 14	6	2 sections at work on 7th Corps line, 1 section in BOIS FAYS superintending cutting parties, bundle making etc., 1 section at ROSSIGNOL Farm making huts, cook houses, ablution benches, covered latrines etc for troops in the training area. Work on water supply at COUIN & COIGNEUX continued.	
	" 29		New work for 300 rifles sited & traced out between works 16 & 17 on 7th Corps line situated V 4 a 5.6. ref. sheet 57d. France 40,000. Started canteen for the men with capital of 500 francs. Goods obtained from E.F.C. Very much appreciated and a great boon to the men saving them from paying exorbitant prices charged in the local villages.	
	" 30		1 section to HEBUTERNE & 1 section to SAILLY	
HEBUTERNE	" 31		2 sections to HEBUTERNE relieving 1st Sn. Dn. Co. R.E. Engaged in usual work, improving & repairing trenches etc.	

Army Form C. 2118

Vol 5 sheet 3.

WAR DIARY
or
INTELLIGENCE SUMMARY.
(Erase heading not required.)

Summary of Events and Information

Extracts from weekly States

Date	Strength Off. O.R.	Reinforcements Off. O.R.	Transfers from to	Hospital from to	Remarks
Oct 2	5 208			1 1	
" 9	6 211	1 1	2*	1 3	* 2 drivers from 1st Bn Div. Co. Res.
" 16	6 211	3		1	
" 23	6 210			2	
" 30	6 208				

Thigh
Major.

121/793

— Confidential —

War Diary

of

2/1 S.M. Field Coy. R.E.

— 48th Div. —

From Nov 1 — to Nov 30 1915.

Volume 6

Army Form C. 2118.

Vol 6 sheet 1.

WAR DIARY
or
INTELLIGENCE SUMMARY.
(Erase heading not required.)

Instructions regarding War Diaries and Intelligence Summaries are contained in F. S. Regs., Part II. and the Staff Manual respectively. Title pages will be prepared in manuscript.

Place	Date	Hour	Summary of Events and Information	Remarks and references to Appendices
	1915			
HEBUTERNE	Nov 16		3 sections engaged on usual front line work. Very wet weather	
	Nov 13.		From Nov 8th to Nov 13th, trenches falling in badly where unrevetted.	
	Nov 7		Major E.T.R. R.G.S. proceeded on 8 days leave to England.	
	" 7		Reinforcement 1 driver reported for duty.	
	" 9		No 2153 Sapper Henry W. wounded in right foot while wiring in front of Battalion reserve line	
	Nov 14		Section from SAILLY, 1st Section from HEBUTERNE to ROSSIGNOL farm	
	" 15		Relieved by 1st S.R. Fd. Co., remaining 2 sections to ROSSIGNOL farm	
ROSSIGNOL	Nov 15 6		2 sections at work on 7th Corps line, which despite the bad weather, is	
farm	Nov 30.		standing well, all firing trenches revetted, owing to lack of material unable to revet communication trenches and it was decided to only keep them open to a depth of 3 feet, maximum size of any new dug outs made to be 8'x6'. All dug outs standing well but entrances fallen in in some cases, owing to them not having been framed. All splinter proof shelters constructed by laying a roll plate about 18" from the edge with light logs across & 9" to 12" of earth on top. Allowed	

Army Form C. 2118.

Vol 6 Sheet 2

WAR DIARY
or
INTELLIGENCE SUMMARY.
(Erase heading not required.)

Place	Date	Hour	Summary of Events and Information	Remarks and references to Appendices
Rosignol Farm	1915 Nov 1st to Nov 30		Owing to the sides falling in 1 section superintending wood cutting & hurdle walling in R.E. Chateau wood. 1 section & details on R.E. services in divisional area. New horse watering & water cart filling place newly completed at Couin. Water pumped from Couin springs. Extracts from weekly strength return.	

Date	Strength Offrs	Strength O.R.	Reinforcements	Transfers	Hospital	C.C.S.	Remarks
Nov. 6	6	208	nil	nil	3	3	
" 13	6	205	1	nil	1	4	1 wounded
" 20	6	203	nil	nil	1	2	
" 27	6	206	3	nil	1	1	

Thiff
Major

Army Form C. 2118.

Vol 7 Sheet 1.

WAR DIARY
or
INTELLIGENCE SUMMARY.
(Erase heading not required.)

Place	Date	Hour	Summary of Events and Information	Remarks and references to Appendices
ROSSIGNOL Farm	1915 Dec 1.		Work on 7th Corps line continued, also horse watering route cut filling place at COUIN. One section to SAILLY & three sections to HEBUTERNE to relieve 1st Sn. H.G.	
HEBUTERNE	Dec 2 to Dec 16.	12.0.	Usual work in front line & R.E. services generally. The continued wet weather caused many trenches to fall in & in places the front line had to be abandoned, small posts being constructed at intervals along the line, usually at the head of communication trenches. Our men areparos were directed towards keeping open communication from front to rear & repairs to dugouts, many of these collapsed, but more frequently the frames held good but the sides, through not being revetted, fell in. Light shelters covered with corrugated iron to give shelter from the weather only, were erected in the front line usually behind traverses. Overland tracks of hurdles & bridges across trenches were laid, where it was impossible to keep open the communication trenches, and these were used to relieve posts in the front line by night. This applied particularly to our right section G. occupied alternately by the 7th Worcesters & 4th Oxfords	

Army Form C. 2118.

vol 7 sheet 2.

WAR DIARY
or
INTELLIGENCE SUMMARY.
(Erase heading not required.)

Place	Date	Hour	Summary of Events and Information	Remarks and references to Appendices
HETSOTERNE	1915 Dec 26.		A considerable amount of revetment to trenches was done & much more could have been done if the supply of material had been adequate, the chief shortage being that of long (9'–8') pickets for securing the revetment to the trenches. The most suitable form of revetment proved to be rabbit wire netting with a backing of straw, flax or other similar material. What is undoubtedly required is a waterproof or rate repelling covering for the sides of a trench. This causes the water to run off & not to soak into the soil & cause it to flake off in layers starting from the bottom. If rabbit wire netting backed with pitch paper issued to the battery could be issued in rolls ready for use, it would be invaluable for revetting purposes & would greatly expedite the work.	
	Dec 4.		No. 13350 Sapper Bubb H.T. Severely wounded by explosion of 8.2" H.E. shell which destroyed a cairn, a portion of our billet.	
	Dec 5. Dec 6.		No. 13350 Sapper Bubb H.T. died in hospital. No. 1519 Cpl. Ashan A. Killed by rifle bullet while carrying line over	

Army Form C. 2118.

Vol 7 Sheet 3

WAR DIARY
or
INTELLIGENCE SUMMARY.
(Erase heading not required)

Instructions regarding War Diaries and Intelligence Summaries are contained in F. S. Regs., Part II. and the Staff Manual respectively. Title pages will be prepared in manuscript.

Place	Date	Hour	Summary of Events and Information	Remarks and references to Appendices
	1915			
HEBUTERNE	Dec 6		Parapet in Battalion reserve trench VAUBAN, in preparation of trenches out the water.	
	Dec 9		1 Sapper reinforcement	
	" 9		3 Sappers reinforcement	
	Dec 16		1 Section from HEBUTERNE + section from SAILLY to ROSSIGNOL	
	" 17		3 sections from HEBUTERNE to ROSSIGNOL, relieved by 1st S.M. Col. Co. RE.	
ROSSIGNOL FARM	Dec 18 to		2 sections at work on 7th Corps line, work confined to repairing trenches.	
	Dec 31		dug outs and keeping drains clear	
			1 section superintending wood cutting & hurdle making in Bois chateau wood France Sqd. J 20 c & d, and small wood at CONGREUX (J 9 C 2.9).	
			1 section completing Cov in watering scheme (open for use Dec 20) + RE. services generally	
	Dec 25. 11.0a		Church service	
	6.0p.		Christmas dinner, goose, plum pudding etc	
	8.0p.		Concert	
	Dec 27 6.30p		Variety entertainment by "VIVACIOUS VARLETS" 1st S.M. Col. Unit.	

1577 Wt.W10791/1773 500,000 1/15 D.D.&L.   A.D.S.S./Forms/C. 2118.

Army Form C. 2118.

Vol 7 Sheet 4

WAR DIARY
or
INTELLIGENCE SUMMARY.
(Erase heading not required.)

Place	Date	Hour	Summary of Events and Information	Remarks and references to Appendices
ROSSIGNOL FARM	1915 Dec 28	4·30p	Cinematograph entertainment by 48th Div. Supply Col.	
	Dec 31	6·30p	3 sections to HOUTKERQUE, 1 section to SMULY. Relieved 1st Bn. 2d. Co.	
	Dec 26		6 Sappers reinforcements.	

EXTRACT from WEEKLY STRENGTH RETURN

Date	Strength Off.	O.R.	REINFORCEMENTS	TRANSFERS	KILLED	C.C.S. From	C.C.S. To	Remarks
Dec 4	6	203	—	2*	—	1	1	1 known to 17th's R.E.
" 11	6	200	4	—	2	—	5	1 Engr to 1st Bn 2d Co Rd.
" 18	6	199	—	—	—	1	2	
" 25	6	199	—	—	—	—	1	

[signature]
O.C. 2/1st Field Co 2d Co R.E.

O.C. 2/1st FIELD COY., S.M.R.E.
46th S. MIDLAND DIVISION
No. ___ Date 8-1-17

CONFIDENTIAL.

WAR DIARY

— of —

2/1 South Midland Field Co. R.E.

48th Division.

from Jan 1 to Jan 31 1916

(Volume 8.)

Army Form C. 2118.

Vol 8 Sheet 1.

WAR DIARY
or
INTELLIGENCE SUMMARY.
(Erase heading not required.)

Place	Date	Hour	Summary of Events and Information	Remarks and references to Appendices
FESUBERT	1916 Jan 1	1	3 sections at work on front line trenches & repairing dug outs etc.	
			1 section at SMILY at work in divisional workshops & R.E. services	
	2		"do"	
	3		Heavy bombardment of front line trenches in H & J sections. (German S7 N.E., K.16d, K.16 & K.16d, 5" direct hits with 5.9" shells in Lateral Communication Trench. WILLOW LANE (K.16d.) Causing Blockages to 6' to 15' long & 2 direct hits on dug out in BUGEAUD fm trench (K.17.c.) in which 15 men were letting shelter. 8 escaped but 7 were killed & buried in the debris.	
			1 section Sappers & infantry working party of 46 mustered from 6pm to 4 am (Jan 4) clearing WILLOW LANE & removing timber & earth burying the men in BUGEAUD dug out. he were successful in reaching the bodies & identifying them but it was not considered desirable to liberate them owing to the labour entailed & they were buried on the spot. Front line trench (BUGEAUD) was badly damaged but posts were continued in small fronts of the damaged portion & the A.D.S. blocked	

1577 Wt W10791/1773 500,000 1/15 D.D. & L.   A.D.S.S./Forms/C. 2118.

Army Form C. 2118.

W L E Sheet 2

WAR DIARY
or
INTELLIGENCE SUMMARY.
(Erase heading not required.)

Instructions regarding War Diaries and Intelligence Summaries are contained in F. S. Regs., Part II. and the Staff Manual respectively. Title pages will be prepared in manuscript.

Place	Date	Hour	Summary of Events and Information	Remarks and references to Appendices
HEBUTERNE	1916 Jan 4.		Usual work Continued.	
	" 5		"	
	" 6		"	
	" 7		"	
	" 11	6	Day fine morning fine, afternoon very wet.	
			Usual work, VER CINGETORIX cleaned + boarded to FORT SUSSEX	Sheet 57 N.E. 30 (Ault B.)
			FORT SOUTH DOWN cleaned + revetted & 1 shelter made good.	K. 22.
			VAUBAN cleaned + partly revetted from VERCINGETORIX to DUGUESCLIN.	
			No 2237 St Bruce H. sent to base for transfer to England for discharge, being a minor American citizen	
	" 12		H.Q's + 3 sections moved from HEBUTERNE to ROSSIGNOL } relieved by	
			1 section " " SAILLY to ROSSIGNOL } 1st Fin. M. C. R.E.	
ROSSIGNOL Farm.	Jan 13	6	2 sections resumed work on 7th Corps line	
	" 24 incl.		1 section superintending hood cutting, Kindle making &c in wood S of CORGNEUX	
			1 section R.E. services generally, making + erecting huts &c near von Kahr's	
			erected at foot of hill below ROSSIGNOL farm on the CORGNEUX – SOUASTRE road.	

WAR DIARY
or
INTELLIGENCE SUMMARY.
(Erase heading not required.)

Army Form C. 2118.

WC 8 sheet 3

Place	Date	Hour	Summary of Events and Information	Remarks and references to Appendices
HEBUTERNE	1916 Jan 25th		3 sections to HEBUTERNE 1 section to SAILLY	
	Jan 31		Majority of the Sappers at HEBUTERNE engaged on mined O.P's for R.A. with dugouts. Three 8 hour shifts worked daily, each shift of 3 men. Average time taken to complete one O.P. 20 days. Sketch attached shows one O.P typical of the rest. The top of the excavation shafts are to be covered with a suitable "camouflage", in most cases a "hot de bois". These are being made at AMIENS. 8 O.P.S in course of construction, situated as below ① R. MAISON K.9.6.6.5. ② Bois POILUS K.9.6.8.3. ③ HADDON K.10.C.8.9 ④ RENAUD K.10.d.3.6. ⑤ GENEVIÈVE K.16.C.7.2. ⑥ PAPIN K.21.a.9.1. ⑦ AUERSTADT K.21.d.1.8. ⑧ WAGRAM K.21.d.25.55. The rest of the Sappers engaged on R.E. services & recovering & revetting trenches VILLARS & VAUBAN. K.22.	57D N.E. 3rd sheets of 2nd edition

Army Form C. 2118.

Vol 8 Sheet 4.

WAR DIARY
or
INTELLIGENCE SUMMARY.
(Erase heading not required.)

EXTRACT from WEEKLY STATES.

Date	Strength Off	OR	Reinforcements	Transfers	Killed	C.C.S. From	To	Remarks
Jan 1	6	204	6	1*	—	—	—	* S/Sgt Cornelius to England for commission
" 8	6	203	—	—	—	—	1	
" 15	6	203	3	1*	—	—	2	* St. Bruce to Base for discharge
" 22	6	200	1	1*	—	—	2	* 1 Sapper to Hosp. P.E.
" 29	6	199	—	1*	—	—	2	* Intermediate training to 1st Sch. Rel. Arts.

Whipp Major
O.C. 2/1st Sn. 2d Co. P.E.

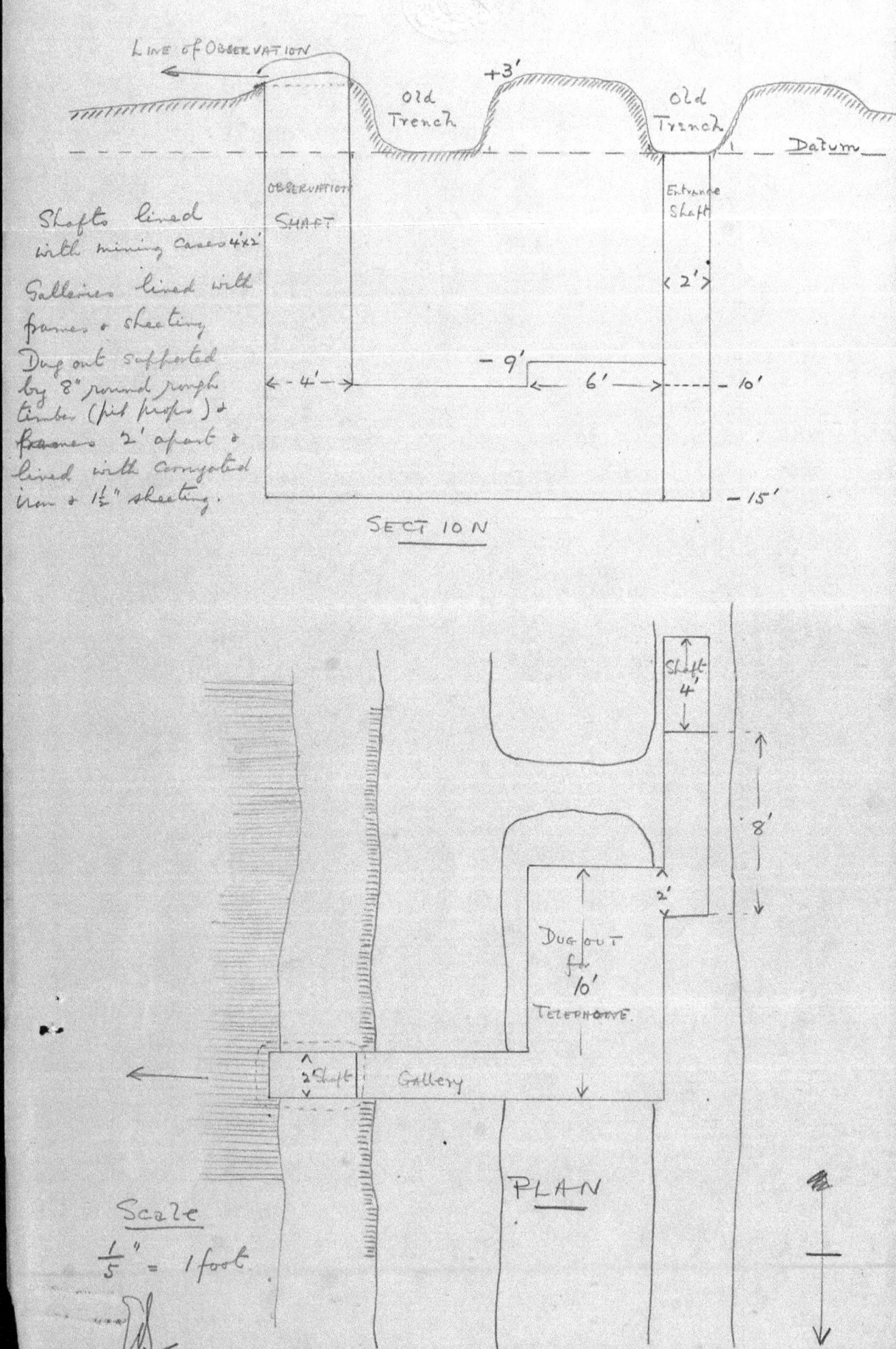

CONFIDENTIAL.

WAR DIARY

-of-

2/1 S.M. Field Company. R.E.

from Feb 1 to Feb 29
1916

(VOLUME 9..)

Army Form C. 2118.

Vol 9 sheet 1.

WAR DIARY
or
INTELLIGENCE SUMMARY.
(Erase heading not required.)

Place	Date	Hour	Summary of Events and Information	Remarks and references to Appendices
	1916.			
HEBUTERNE	Feb. 1. 6		3 sections at HEBUTERNE engaged on mixed OP's for R.A., clearing and revetting trenches. VILLERS & FAUBAN & R.E. work generally	
	Feb. 9.		1 section at SAILLY repairing roads & billets etc.	
	Feb. 8.		No 2078 Sapper G.R. Miller & No 2169 Sapper E.G. Combs killed in trench FAUBAN R22.6.1.1. by H.E. shell while engaged in clearing & revetting the trench. No 1726 Sapper C. Cave slightly wounded by splinter of wood at same time.	
	Feb. 9		3 section from HEBUTERNE to ROSSIGNOL farm, relieved by 1/4 Bn 2/Co	
ROSSIGNOL	Feb. 10		23 reinforcements arrived from Base.	
	Feb. 13		HQ's, 1 section of Sappers & all horses & transport moved to SOUASTRE. 3 section of Sappers to BIENVILLERS, relieving 153rd 2d C. R.E. on trenches 58.to 76 inclusive the 144 & D.g. hole. taking over portion of 37th Div: line. E22.d & E11.a. (57 & NE 112/sec)	
BIENVILLERS & SOUASTRE	Feb. 13. 6 to Feb. 28.		3 sections at BIENVILLERS engaged on front line work, making shelters erecting tubular shelters, revetting trench from 74 to TRENCHED to PONQUEVILLERS. E 16.11 & E 15.d. 6.0 1 section at SOUASTRE engaged on R.E. stores & making frames etc for dugouts.	

1577 Wt.W10791/1773 500,000 1/15 D.D.&L. A.D.S.S./Forms/C. 2118.

WAR DIARY
or
INTELLIGENCE SUMMARY.

Army Form C. 2118.

Vol 9 sheet 2

Place	Date	Hour	Summary of Events and Information	Remarks and references to Appendices
BIEZVILLERS	19.6 Feb 23.		Front line trench 55 & between trenches 55 & 54 strongly wired by sappers after German attack on trench 55.	
	Feb 29.		3 sections BIEZVILLERS to ROSSIGNOL farm in 144 & 2cf. role being relieved by portion of 37th Divl. HQ's + 1 section at SOUASTRE	

EXTRACT from WEEKLY STATES.

Date 1916	Stamped Offs. OR.	Reinforcements Offs. OR.	Transfers	KILLED	C.C.S. From To	Remarks
Feb 5	6 197	— —	—	—	1 1	
" 12	7 215	1° 23	1	2	— 4	× 1 driver from 1/2 nd Sn. H. Co. ⊙ 2nd Lt Richardson reported on journey
" 19	7 220	— 3	1	1	2 2	
" 26	7 218	— 1	1	1	1 2	

[signature]
Major
O.C. 2/1st Sth Mid Divl. Corps

CONFIDENTIAL.

WAR DIARY

of

2/1 South Midland Field Co. R.E. (T.)

from 1st March 1916   to 31st March 1916

(Volume 10)

Army Form C. 2118

Vol 10 sheet 1.

WAR DIARY
or
INTELLIGENCE SUMMARY
(Erase heading not required.)

Instructions regarding War Diaries and Intelligence Summaries are contained in F.S. Regs., Part II. and the Staff Manual respectively. Title Pages will be prepared in manuscript.

Place	Date	Hour	Summary of Events and Information	Remarks and references to Appendices
SOUASTRE	1916 March 1.		Hq's + No 1 section at SOUASTRE Nos 2 3 + 4 sections at ROSSIGNOL farm. Equipment & stores overhauled & necessary repairs done.	
"	"	2.	Bridging equipment & all spare stores to ROSSIGNOL farm.	
"	"	3.	Hq's + Nos 2 + 3 sections to COZINCAMPS. Nos 1 + 4 sections to COURCELLES } Relieving the 9th W. Co. R.E. who left with the 12th Inf Bde on their portion of the line being taken over by the 144th Inf Bde.	
COZINCAMPS	"	4.	Nos 1 + 4 sections working in workshops at COURCELLES. No 2 section working in area held alternately by 4th & 6th Som. battln trenches from K 29 c 8.8. to K 23 d 3.0. No 3 section working in area held alternately by 7th & 8th Wor.s. battln trenches from K 35 a 4.4. to K 29 c 8.8. Special items of work engaged upon (a). Water supply from SUCRERIE K 33 d. supplying front line system held by 144th Inf. Bde. also the 36th Divn on our right. Engine & pump renewed in and rendered shell proof. Water supply track to COZINCAMPS from the SUCRERIE completed. (b). Erection of steel tubular shelters in BAIZIM wood K 28 C. 6.4. OBSERVATION wood K 28 6. 3.3. + the SUCRERIE. (c) Shell proof O.P.'s with steel rail & concrete roofs for R.A. at K 21 C 9.0. K 33 G 55.75. and K 34 a 8.3	

1875 Wt. W593/826 1,000,000 4/15 J.B.C. & A. A.D.S.S./Forms/C. 2118.

Army Form C. 2118

Vol 10 sheet 2

WAR DIARY
or
INTELLIGENCE SUMMARY
(Erase heading not required.)

Instructions regarding War Diaries and Intelligence Summaries are contained in F.S. Regs., Part II. and the Staff Manual respectively. Title Pages will be prepared in manuscript.

Place	Date	Hour	Summary of Events and Information	Remarks and references to Appendices
COLINCAMPS	1916 Mar 4.		(d). Completion & upkeep of Divisional 2nd line HITTITE & PALESTINE from K33 6 8.1 to K21 d 15,20.	
			(e) Construction of Keeps at "ZOLLTREYSTEATS" K33 d 3.1 BASIN MOAT K28 c 6.4. & ELLES SQUARE about K33 6 3.1	
"do"	Mar 19 2.25a.		Received orders to "Stand To" with 2 sections at COLINCAMPS, heavy enemy bombardment of our front line	
	2.40a.		2 sections ready to move	
	3.15a.		Received orders to "Stand down". All quiet.	
do.	March 27		Second engine in SUCKERIE placed in position in Elephant Dugout & given trial run.	
	" 28		Spot engine in SUCKERIE broke big end both fracturing crankcase, piston connecting rod. Water supply carried on successfully by other engine	
	" 30		No 4 section moved to COIGN to complete hutting camp arrangements for new Divisional HQ Battalion in rest.	

1875 Wt. W593/826 1,000,000 4/15 J.B.C. & A. A.D.S.S./Forms/C. 2118.

Army Form C. 2118

Volume 10 sheet 3

WAR DIARY
or
INTELLIGENCE SUMMARY
(Erase heading not required.)

Place	Date	Hour	Summary of Events and Information	Remarks and references to Appendices
COLINCAMPS.	March 31.		Enemy shelled W end COLINCAMPS, probably searching for 9.2 position just in rear of billet. Very accurate & rapid shooting with no effect on battery. 2 direct hits on billet, man wounded & foot cart smashed. Billet adjoining but several times with incendiary shells was completely destroyed.	

Extract from Weekly States

Date 1916.	Strength Off.	OR.	Reinforcements. Off.	OR.	Transfers.	Killed	C C S From.	To.	Remarks.
March 4.	7	219	-	-	-	1	1	-	
11	7	218	-	-	-	1×	-	-	×Sick M.T. CCS
18	7	212	-	-	5⊙	-	-	-	⊙ Divisional Salvage Co.
25	7	211	-	-	-	-	1	1	

T.M.W. Crawford Capt.
OC 2/1 SM Field ERE

CONFIDENTIAL.

WAR DIARY

— of —

2/1 South Midland Field Co. R.E.

from April 1 to 30th
1916

(Volume 11)

WAR DIARY or INTELLIGENCE SUMMARY

Army Form C. 2118

VOLUME II Sheet 1.

Place	Date	Hour	Summary of Events and Information	Remarks and references to Appendices
COLINCAMPS.	April 2nd.		No 1 section moved from COURCELLES to SAILLY handing over R.E. stores to a section of 223rd Field Co. Nos 2 & 3 sections moved to HEBUTERNE; thence HQ moved to SAILLY. Thus completing unit's move. All work in sector was handed over to 223rd Field Co. with the exception of water supply at SUCERIE which was taken over by Royal Anglesea Siege Co. R.E.	
SAILLY-au-BOIS.	3rd.		Work started in G.F. sector, No 2 section being detailed for Brigade work, principally in clearing, making good communication trenches. Nos 1 & 3 were started on infantry & Artillery O.P's about K.23.a.7228, K.21.a.9108, K.21.b.4061, K.21.b.3250, K.21.b.1207, K.16.c.0121	51° NE 3 & 4 parts of 2nd edition
	5th.		No 4 section returned from COUIN.	
	7th.		Old french trench running parallel to PAPIN (HEBUTERNE - SUCERIE road) was carefully cleaned so as to show no trace of recent work & two mined communication trenches were started at K.21.b.0560 to connect from PAPIN.	

Army Form C. 2118

WAR DIARY
or
INTELLIGENCE SUMMARY
(Erase heading not required.)

Vol 11. Sheet 2.

Place	Date	Hour	Summary of Events and Information	Remarks and references to Appendices
SAILLY-au-BOIS	April 9th		Erected dugouts for HQ for Right Battalion in TROSSACHS. Dugout made in units of 9' as per sketch. 4 units in all supplied. K 22 d 2020	
do	"	13th	Work progressing favourably. Not yet from inoculation.	
do	"	17th	CSM Entwistle left and took on RSM to CRE 48th Div. His services were of great assistance, especially in the early days of the Company.	
do	"	21st	OPs at K 21 b 4061, K 21 b 3250 were completed for observation: much dugouts were commenced for extra telephonists etc. Pipe line completed between OBSERVATION WOOD & STAFF COPSE (both K 23 b) & tanks in STAFF COPSE filled. Heard later that this area was to be taken over by 31st Division.	
do	"	22	Major E. BRIGGS returned from leave. Work as above continued. Nos 1, 3 + 4 sections engaged on O.P's for R.A. & Inf. Boles. No 2 section in the line, cleaning & repairing trenches.	

Army Form C. 2118

WAR DIARY
or
INTELLIGENCE SUMMARY
(Erase heading not required.)

Vol II sheet 3.

Summary of Events and Information

Extracts from Weekly States

Date 1916	Strength Off. O.R's	Reinforcements Off. O.R.	Transfers Off. O.R.	Killed	C.C.S. From To	Remarks and references to Appendices
April 1	7 207	— —	— 1ˣ	—	— 3°	Remarks. × Driver Kendal to base for discharge on expiration of service. ○ N° 1571 Sapr Mackham J. wounded.
" 8	7 229	— 22	— 1ˣ	1	1 1	ˣ N° 1354 Sgt Gabriel to bin Salvage Co
" 15	7 226	— —	— —	1	— 3	
" 22	7 229	— 5	— 1ˣ	1	1 2	ˣ Clm Entwistle to Hq R.E. 48ᵗʰ Div
" 29	7 228	— —	— —	1	1 1	as R.S.M.

O.C. 2/1st S.M. Field Coy., R.E.

[stamp: 2/1st S.M. FIELD Coy., R.E. No. Date 1-5-16 48th DIVISION]

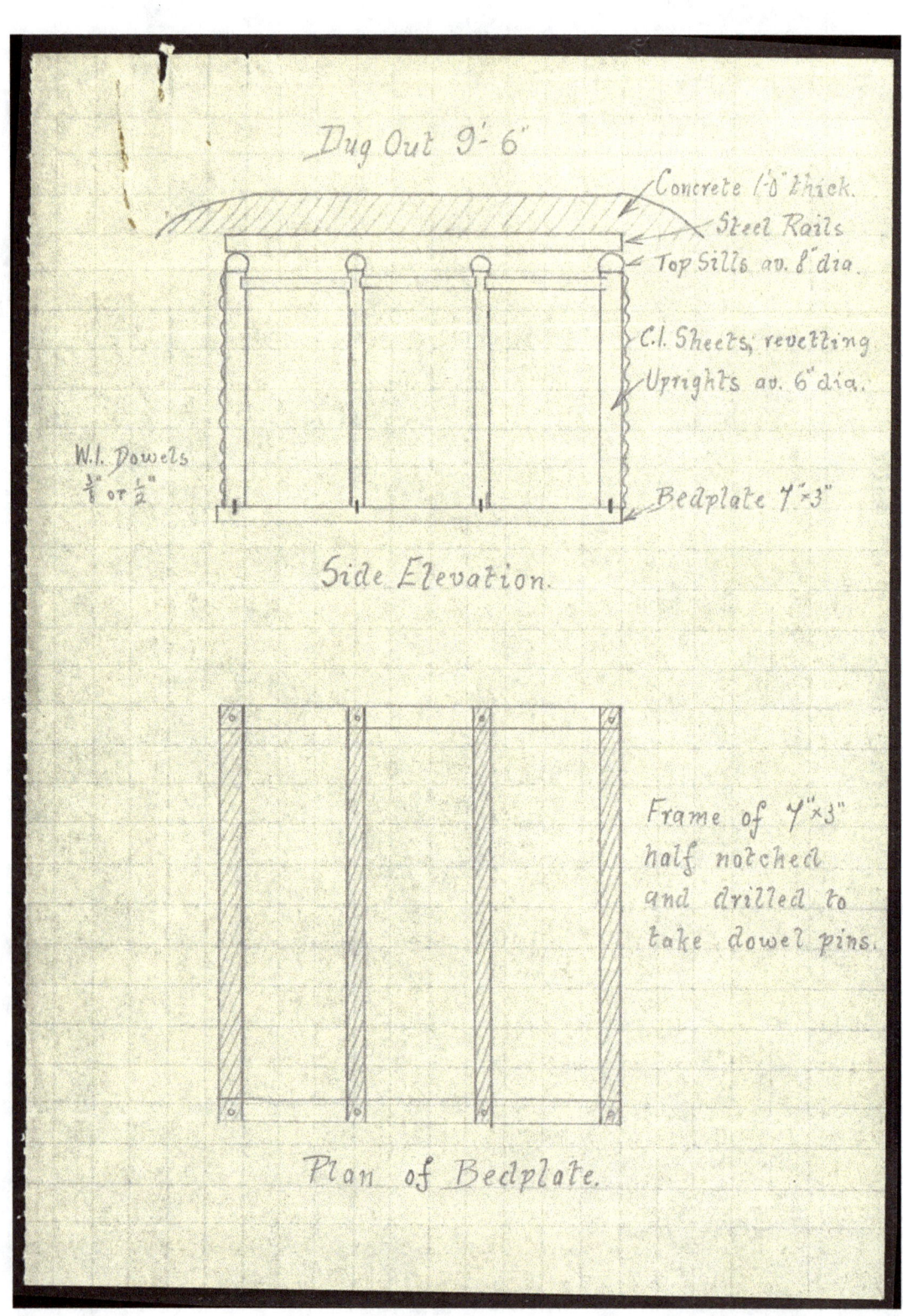

CONFIDENTIAL.

WAR DIARY

— of —

2/1 South Midland Field Company. R.E.

from May 1 to 31

1916

(Volume 12.)

WAR DIARY
or
INTELLIGENCE SUMMARY
(Erase heading not required.)

Army Form C. 2118

Vol 12. Sheet 1

Instructions regarding War Diaries and Intelligence Summaries are contained in F. S. Regs., Part II. and the Staff Manual respectively. Title Pages will be prepared in manuscript.

Place	Date	Hour	Summary of Events and Information	Remarks and references to Appendices
SAILLY-AU-BOIS	1916 May 1		Work in O.P.'s continued by Nos 1 3 & 4 sections. No 2 section on Bde work	
	" 3	10-30 a.m	All 4 sections moved to ROSSIGNOL farm where the Company concentrated. Relieved in line by 1/1st S.M. Fd. Co. R.E.	
ROSSIGNOL farm	" 4	5-15 a	The whole Company together with the bridging equipment of the 1/1st & 1/2nd S.M. Fd Co's moved to DOULLENS. A B C France 574. 40,000 to HEM, 2 miles N of DOULLENS.	
		10-15 a	Move complete after a march of 14 miles. Nly 2 men fell out, both after doing 9 miles. Quite a good performance after 12 months of trench work.	
HEM	" 5 to " 14		Company training, close order drill rifle exercises etc. 6-30 am to 7-30 am. Pontooning, trestle & other bridging, Engineer reconnaissance 8-30 am to 2 pm.	
	" 15	7-0 am	Moved back to ROSSIGNOL farm. Bridging equipment left at HEM for use of 2nd S.M. Fd. Co.	
		11-30 a.m	Move complete	
ROSSIGNOL farm	" 16		Took over stores from 1st Fd. Co.	
	" 17		2 sections moved to SAILLY & took over front line work at HEBUTERNE to Gallets, available at HEBUTERNE; relieved taken by 57th Div	

Army Form C. 2118

vol 12 sheet 2

WAR DIARY
or
INTELLIGENCE SUMMARY
(Erase heading not required.)

Place	Date	Hour	Summary of Events and Information	Remarks and references to Appendices
ROSSIGNOL Farm	1916 May 17	10 p.m.	Taped out new support trench for new front line trench K.17. from junction of PAS de TR & VILLON LANE K.16.d.8.9 & PUISIEUX road K.16.88. Infantry officers the working parties shown parties to new trench & tracing explained.	
"	18	9.30 p.	Work started on new trench & 2 communication trenches to front line & 1 back to our old front line.	
			915 yds of trench in all including traverses 1720 yds of digging Trench dug 5' wide at top & 3' at bottom, 3' deep = 14 sq. ft. Strength of digging party 650 & 1 section of sappers supervising = 80 cu. ft. per man Digging complete.	
"	19 2-0 p.			

1875 Wt. W3593/826 1,000,000 4/15 J.B.C. & A. A.D.S.S./Forms/C. 2118.

Army Form C. 2118

Vol 12 Sheet 3.

WAR DIARY
or
INTELLIGENCE SUMMARY
(Erase heading not required.)

Place	Date	Hour	Summary of Events and Information	Remarks and references to Appendices
ROSSIGNOL Farm	1916 May 18		The working party was supplied by 7th Munsters & the practice of the work & arrangements made were explained to all their Company Officers in the afternoon. The whole battalion turned out & everything went without a hitch. Casualties nil, though it was a bright moonlight night and the work was within 600 yds of the German front line.	
	" 19	1.30 am	The whole of the tunnel was wired with a fence with double apron & 2 rows of French Concertina work	
	" 19	to	The 4th Gloucesters supplied a wiring party of 100 men & a carrying party of another 100 men, 1 section of sappers supervising & assisting. Casualties 1 man of 4th Glos wounded. Wiring completed.	
	" 20		The whole was a most satisfactory piece of work.	
			Work continued on above trench, deepening & revetting	
			O.P.'s & Heavy T.M. emplacements constructed.	
	" 25	11 pm	Work on dugouts for telephone exchanges at junctions of buried cables Support trench to front line trenches K 23(c-10) sited & travel out, between JETTA & JEAN BART, 750 yds of travel to be dug and wired.	

Army Form C. 2118

Vol 12 Sheet 4.

WAR DIARY
or
INTELLIGENCE SUMMARY
(Erase heading not required.)

Instructions regarding War Diaries and Intelligence Summaries are contained in F.S. Regs, Part II. and the Staff Manual respectively. Title Pages will be prepared in manuscript.

Place	Date	Hour	Summary of Events and Information	Remarks and references to Appendices
1916 ROSSIGNOL FARM	May 27		Working party of 450 men from 8th Norse funded for digging & wiring. Altho' the same precautions were taken & preliminary Explanations made as in the case of trench dug on May 18th, the work done was most unsatisfactory, only 300 yds of the trench had been dug to depths ranging from 3' to 1'6" & the wiring was very poor.	
"	28	10 pm	Work started at 10 p.m. & carried out 2/1 m. Casualties nil	
"	30		Work continued as above trench, whole length completed but not to full depth. Wire was continued but not complete. The company, there mounted section, moved into bivouacs at J.17.c.1.5. Mr. J.T. MILEY, being relieved of work in the front line and at R.E. Stores COGNEUX by 2nd F.M. Pl. Co. R.E. Move complete	
SAILLY	31	4-0 pm	Work on O.P.'s & company continued. Telephone exchange dugouts. "30" "do" Sites selected for deep dug-outs & preliminary work started. 2 behind PORT GROSVENOR K21a, 2 off AVERSTADT K21a 7.1. 1 off WRANGLE K23a 9.2. 2 at 3rd Barricade K17c 3.2	

Army Form C. 2118

Vol 12 sheet 5

WAR DIARY
or
INTELLIGENCE SUMMARY
(Erase heading not required.)

Summary of Events and Information

EXTRACTS from WEEKLY STATES

Date 1916	Strength Offs.	O.R.	Reinforce Offs.	O.R.	Transfers Offs.	O.R.	Killed	Cas From	To	Remarks and references to Appendices
May 6.	6	225	—	—	1*	—	—	—	3	× I/Lt. Richardson to England for training
" 13	6	223	—	—	—	1*	—	1	2	× 1461 Spr Butler T.E. to 4th Div. Salvage Co.
" 20	6	223	—	—	—	1	—	1	1	
" 27	6	223	—	—	1	1	—	1	1	

D. Wigg
Major
OC 2/1st Fm. 2d Co. R.E.

CONFIDENTIAL.

WAR DIARY

of

2/1 South Midland Field Co. R.E.

From 1st June 1916 to 30th June 1916.

(Volume 13)

Army Form C. 2118

Vol 13 Sheet 1

WAR DIARY
or
INTELLIGENCE SUMMARY
(Erase heading not required.)

Place	Date	Hour	Summary of Events and Information	Remarks and references to Appendices
SAILLY	1916 June 1		Preliminary work on trenches for deep dug outs continued.	
	" 2	5-30a	The Company proceeded by march route to HEM. for training in pontooning, trestle bridging, etc.	
		11-0a	have complete.	
HEM	June 3 to 10		Engaged in pontooning, trestle bridging, formed trestle bridging etc. No 3 Section erected a trestle bridge to carry 5 cwt per foot run live load across the R. ANCRE. Length of bridge 60', each bay 10', roadway 9'. Spars 10"/12" for transoms & 7"/8" for legs. All material on the site. Time taken including ramps at each end (abt 10' long) & provision of hand rails, screens etc. 420 man hours. Av. number of men working 15 for 7 hrs for 4 days.	
HEM.	" 11	7-0a	No 3 Section to LOUVENCOURT for work on roads under CE VIII Corps	
		11-0a	HQ's + Nos 1+2 Sections to ROSSIGNOL	
		11-20a	No 3 Section have complete	
		4-15p	HQ's + Nos 1+2 Sectns move complete	

Army Form C. 2118

WAR DIARY
or
INTELLIGENCE SUMMARY
(Erase heading not required.)

Vol 13 sheet 2.

Place	Date	Hour	Summary of Events and Information	Remarks and references to Appendices
HEM	1916 June 11		No 4 Section remained at HEM to dismount the bridges & hook pontoons & trestle wagons.	
ROSSIGNOL	" 12		Took over stores from 2nd S. Mid. Fd. Co.	
	" 13		No 4 Section moved from HEM to ROSSIGNOL with all 3 companies bridging equipment.	
			No 3 section returned.	
	" 15/16.		A party of sappers, Cpl Cox, Sappers Askew, Bryan, Sage, Richardson and Paine all from No 1 section made an attempt to cut the German wire at K 23 a 1.9 with Bangalore torpedoes to make way for a raiding party of the 7t Worcs. The wire at this point had been reconnoitred previously & was very strong & estimated at 20 to 30 yds deep. 6 Bangalore torpedoes each 14 feet long were prepared, fitted with ammonal & fitted with a hells grenade adapted as a firing device. There was no artillery bombardment, but the R.A. kept up intermittent firing on a wide section of the German front line so as to disguise the explosion of the torpedoes.	

WAR DIARY or INTELLIGENCE SUMMARY

Army Form C. 2118

Vol 13 Sheet 3.

Place	Date	Hour	Summary of Events and Information	Remarks and references to Appendices
ROSSIGNOL	1916 June 25/16		Each man carried out one torpedo & on arrival at the German wire dumped their torpedoes, afterwards carrying them up to the wire & placing them in position working in pairs, each pair laying 1 before firing it in succession. The 1st, 2nd torpedoes exploded successfully, the 3rd failed & a 4th was carried up & laid alongside it, this exploded & is believed to have also exploded the 3rd one which originally failed. About 14 yards of wire were now cut leaving a clear gap about 12 feet wide. It was found there was a gap between the belt of wire cut & the next belt. The 5th torpedo was carried up & exploded but the 2 men firing it either lost their way & did not get clear in time & were wounded by the explosion. They were carried back to our own lines. The 6th torpedo was laid with its nose resting on the German parapet but it failed to explode. About this time 3 of the remaining 4 of the parties were wounded Allis' the attempt was unsuccessful the party had made a	

Army Form C. 2118

vol 13 sheet 4

WAR DIARY
or
INTELLIGENCE SUMMARY
(Erase heading not required.)

Place	Date	Hour	Summary of Events and Information	Remarks and references to Appendices
ROSSIGNOL	1916 June 15/16		Very gallant & spirited attempt & were warmly commended for their efforts by Major General FANSHAWE Commanding the 48th Division & great credit were given to them all. The trumpler Exploders were made up & fused & fitted with detonators 3 weeks before the raid actually took place tho' it was originally contemplated using them the same night & I consider the failure of 2 of them to be due to the Exploders getting damp. No. 3 section returned to ROSSIGNOL from LOUVENCOURT.	
	June 21 June 1/6 " 30		Very hard at work in stores making frames for deep dugouts, gallery frames & cases, hand bombs etc. required in front line. Over 30 tons of material nearly manufactured in the stores were sent up to the front line each day for 10 days.	

Army Form C. 2118

vol 13 sheet 5

WAR DIARY
or
INTELLIGENCE SUMMARY
(Erase heading not required.)

Summary of Events and Information

EXTRACTS from WEEKLY STATES

Date	Place	Hour	Strength Off. men OR.	Reinforcements	Transfers From To	Killed	C.C.S. From To	Remarks and references to Appendices
1916 June 3			6 224	—	3 —	1	— 2	* 2587 Pte Williams from 1/4th Glos. 2909 1/4 Spr Apperes from 2nd Sect Salop G. 2094 Spr Asley from 1/1st Pn 2d Co.
" 10			6 224	—	— —	—	1 —	
" 17			6 217	—	— —	1	1 7	
" 24			6 220	2*	— —	1	— 1	* Transferred in to field. No 3057 L. Cpl Ratfield from the base.

3'd ties for R.E.

2/1 S.M.? Coy Vol 14 Sheet 1

WAR DIARY
or
INTELLIGENCE SUMMARY

Army Form C. 2118

Place	Date	Hour	Summary of Events and Information	Remarks and references to Appendices
ROSSIGNOL FARM	1/7/16	11.30am	Passed starting point T15c35. Proceeded to billets P18a96 arriving 2.10pm	Trench Map 57D SE 2b 1/20,000
MAILLY-MAILLET	2nd		Made reconnaissance of front line from Q17c - Q16b & approached heads with a view to siting communication trenches to open up into German line	
		8pm	Lt WATTS & 12 sappers from No 1 section left to trace out line from Q17a T2 to Q17a 54 a.o. a starting point for proposed attack of 144th Brigade.	
		8.30pm	Received orders to move at 3.15am to ENGLEBELMER await orders	
		11.20pm	Received notice that all operations concerning 48th Division were cancelled.	
"	3rd	3.30pm	Orders to move back to billets occupied on the 1st. Passed starting point 7.0pm arriving ROSSIGNOL FARM 9.20pm	
ROSSIGNOL	4th	8.30p	2 sections to COURCELLES arrived 10*pm	
	5th	8.0a	2 sections & dugouts at COL IN CAMPS Hqs of company at COURCELLES. Reconnoitred the COL IN CAMPS sector handed over by the 31st Div to 48th Div. & started work of cleaning trenches &c.	
			1 section engaged on work at R.E. store COURCELLES.	
			1 section " " night work, repairs to tramline, water supply &	
			2 sections " " heavy shifts on deep dugouts, with cleaning communication & fire trenches.	

Army Form C. 2118

vol 14 sheet 2.

WAR DIARY
or
INTELLIGENCE SUMMARY
(Erase heading not required.)

Place	Date	Hour	Summary of Events and Information	Remarks and references to Appendices
COURCELLES	1916 July 6 6/14	6	Work continued as above. Tram line repaired & water supply made good. Good progress made on cleaning trenches. BLENEAU cleaned, graded, boarded & drained from SACKVILLE ST. to MONK. FLAG cleaned up to MONK. EXCEMA cleaned & boarded to ROBROY. LECHATEAU cleaned to 30 yds past ROBROY. JORDAN cleaned & ROB ROY. All the above work done by R.E.'s. In addition to this daily practice of Sussex Pioneers & 5th R. Warwicks worked under R.E. supervision on the new communication trench & lateral communication trenches up to the Battalion Reserve Line. Mined tunnel trenches were recommenced. A strong point at the head of BLENEAU just behind the front line was taped out but no work started. The front line except for the portion between MATTHEW COPSE & MARK COPSE was in a deplorable condition & quite impossible to repair owing to damage by shell fire & the presence of corpses.	
	" 10		2nd Lt. A.G. MACLENNAN of the EAST ANGLIAN FIELD C.O. R.E. joined the Company as reinforcement officer.	
	" 15		Handed over work to 151 Field Co. R.E. 2 sections of this Field Company remaining with them for 2 days.	

WAR DIARY
or
INTELLIGENCE SUMMARY
(Erase heading not required.)

Army Form C. 2118

Vol 14 Sheet 3

Place	Date	Hour	Summary of Events and Information	Remarks and references to Appendices
	1916			
COURCELLES	July 15	12.30 pm	HQ's and 2 sections moved to BOUZINCOURT arriving at 4.5 pm.	
	" 16	1.40 pm	HQ's & 1 section to AVELUY to billets of 206 Col. C. RE. HQ's & 1 section to CRUCIFIX CORNER " 219 " " Horses & transport to MART IN S ART	LA BOISELLE 1/5000.
AVELUY	" 17	7.0 pm	2 sections left at COLINCAMPS arrived march into billets 1 section CRUCIFIX CORNER employed consolidating 1 section AVELUY. 2 sections 4 Co. 5th R Sussex Regt. employed digging communications to join old German front line via WESTLAND TRENCH from X7 b 36 to X1 b 99, X8a 35 - 88, X8a 67 - 93, X2c 71 - 2a 02 by RE & X2a 02 - 2a 10 - 2a 44 by 5th Sussex.	
do.	" 18	8 pm	3 sections RE employed, each with a platoon of sussex. No 4 from X 8a 50 - 35, No 3 from X 2 c12 - 62. No 2 section on WESTLAND TRENCH. Work on this much has much hampered near old German front line owing to number of shell holes & old wire. Motor lorse lines to BOUZINCOURT owing to their being shelled at MARTINSART. Lost 8 horses killed etc.	

Army Form C. 2118
Vol 14 sheet 4

WAR DIARY
or
INTELLIGENCE SUMMARY
(Erase heading not required.)

Place	Date	Hour	Summary of Events and Information	Remarks and references to Appendices
AVELUY	19/20		3 sections RE were employed each with a platoon of Sussex. 85 - 88 - 92 was cleaned out & made passable. 02 - 26 was consolidated & traversed the original German front line from 05 - 09 cleaned out & barricades removed. Portions of all these trenches had to be redone during the night as they were blown in by shell fire. 11 - 59 was also cleaned & firebays made. DOBBIN St - that portion between WESTLAND & German front line - was completed. 1 Platoon Sussex cleaned out RUNINGTON TUNNEL from X.7. b. 62. - X.8. a. 04. latter end was later blown in again.	
"	20/21	4am	Several RE Sussex parties. 1 section RE & 1 Co Sussex worked on keep in OVILLERS & village cleaning out trenches. Remaining sections cleared 26.47 41-59 where damage during the day fulls work could be done much to attack by 144 Inf Brigade.	
"	21/22	4am	Communication trench dug from 91 - 85 to give easy access to right sector. 11-59-71 was cleaned more damage by shell fire & firebays. OVILLERS KEEP was worked on N+E facts on A50. Trenches on N side cleaned MG position made. 2 suffered ms	

Army Form C. 2118

Vol 14 sheet 5

WAR DIARY
or
INTELLIGENCE SUMMARY
(Erase heading not required.)

Place	Date	Hour	Summary of Events and Information	Remarks and references to Appendices
AVELUY	22/23	4 am	2 Platoons were ordered to assist 6th Glos who were attacking 90-40. 2 Sections 1 Co Sussex on reserve. OVILLERS POST. 1 Lt BRIGGS taped line from 47 to him. Trench due E to 200" as assembly point. No 3 section under Lt MATTS was to accompany that man consolidate positions won. This attack failed before reaching Germans position. The services of R.E. were not required. 1 Sapper killed Lt MATTS + 6 sappers wounded. Later when say 1 section was attached to 145 Inf Brigade were sent to consolidate T.9 but as attacks by WARWICKS made no progress, were unable to start. 1 section + 1 Co of platoon Sussex dug 200" transverse fire trench from X 3 c of westward as support line. Trench 9mm to 2' 6" much delayed by hostile MGs, shell fire. Some casualties to Sussex.	
"	23/24	4 am	No parade Lt Robinson then section	
"	24	9 am	2 sections consolidating 144 th Brigade line. 44-47. 02-10-44. 11-24-37.	

1875 Wt. W593/826 1,000,000 4/15 J.B.C. & A. A.D.S.S./Forms/C. 2118.

Army Form C. 2118

Vol 14 Sheet 6

WAR DIARY
or
INTELLIGENCE SUMMARY
(Erase heading not required.)

Place	Date	Hour	Summary of Events and Information	Remarks and references to Appendices
HEBUTERNE	24/25	4am	2 sections R.E. + 1 Co Sussex completed traverses for trench for 200 x W of x 3c O.T. + also 100 x SE of this point.	
"	25/26		1 section took down leaking canvas water tank at CRUCIFIX CORNER, replaced with galvanised tank, made all necessary connections. 2 sections + 1 platoon Sussex started new strong point at 19. Dug out practically new sunken trench from 88 to mature 20 x I/61. Cleared disused 18 - 02. 1 section 3 platoons Sussex constructing supporting points in OUILLERS KEEP	
"	26/27	"	4 sections R.E. + 1 Co Sussex employed also 2 sections 87th F.Co 5th Sussex on construction of strong point 87th F.Co. who had come to take over. 1 section 3rd F.Co, 1 Co 5th Sussex + section 87th F.Co on supporting line N of OUILLERS 2 sections 3rd F.Co + 1/2 section 87th F.Co on strong point at 19. 1 section " + " " on " " + rifle firing site. Both latter positions were bombarded by shell, rifle + rifle firing fire.	

Army Form C. 2118

Vol 14 Sheet 7

WAR DIARY
or
INTELLIGENCE SUMMARY
(Erase heading not required.)

Place	Date	Hour	Summary of Events and Information	Remarks and references to Appendices
MELVY	27/28	4 am	The whole company was employed on wiring the front of trench running from 47 to OVILLERS-POZIERES road then SE to junction of O2-T9, a distance of 500x. About 400x of this trench was wired with a fence 9'×6' apron enclosing 2 rows of concertina wire. All stores for the purpose had to be carried by coolee labour a distance of 1/2 mile.	
"	28/29	"	3 sections employed completing wiring on trench from 47 also deepening & widening from 3'×3' to 4'6"×4'6". This was only practic. as a working party from 12th Division was eng. during the previous night, a series of holes up to 6' deep.	
"	29		Dismounted portion of company moved by bus to DOMQUEUR, NW of DOULLENS, having over to 91 th Field CRE, 12th Division. Transport & 30 HQ Pk Co. & Sth Sussex marched by road to THIEVRES thence to DOMQUEUR arriving at 2 pm on 30th.	LENS 11 1/100,000

Army Form C. 2118

Vol 14 sheet 8.

WAR DIARY
or
INTELLIGENCE SUMMARY
(Erase heading not required.)

Instructions regarding War Diaries and Intelligence Summaries are contained in F.S. Regs., Part II. and the Staff Manual respectively. Title Pages will be prepared in manuscript.

Place	Date	Hour	Summary of Events and Information	Remarks and references to Appendices
Domqueur	31		Resting.	
			EXTRACT FROM WEEKLY STATE	
			STRENGTH. REINFORCEMENTS. TRANSFERS. KILLED. CCS	
			OFF. OR. OFF. OR. From To. From To.	
	June 8	15	6 210 - - - - - - - -	
		22	7 215 1 - - - - - - -	
		29	7 213 - - - 1 off.× - 1 - 1	
			5 202 - - - 1 or.× 1 off. 9 or. 5	× 8th Corps Hq.

M.M. Cumbro
Capt.

48th Divisional Engineers

2/1st SOUTH MIDLAND FIELD COMPANY R. E.

AUGUST 1 9 1 6

Vol. 15 Sheet 1.

INTELLIGENCE SUMMARY

Summaries are contained in F.S. Regs., Part II. and the Staff Manual respectively. Title Pages will be prepared in manuscript.

(Erase heading not required.)

Place	Date	Hour	Summary of Events and Information	Remarks and references to Appendices
Shaps. Aug 3 Domqueur	3	8pm	Dismounted platoon moved to bivouacs at Caesar's Camp near L'Etoile for bivouacs	SHEETS 11 1/100,000
"	8	8pm	Company moved to LONGVILLERS arriving 7.5 pm	do " "
Longvillers	9	5.45 am	Marched to AUTHEULE arriving 1 pm	
Autheule	10	5.30 am	Marched to ACHEUX arriving 11.45 a.m.	
Belleville Acheux	13	5.30 am	1 section pall transport moved to bivouacs near SENLIS, remained 3 section to bivouacs at AVELUY	
Aveluy	15	5 am	2 sections employed on trench back from X 8 b 69 to join X 3 c 19. 1 Section on Brigade HQ dugout at W 12 b 44. 130' of trench boards, road cleared + material carried to pits.	
	16	5 am	1200' trench carried up, trench bullets opened towards X 3 c 88.	

1875 Wt. W593/826 1,000,000 4/15 J.B.C. & A. A.D.S.S./Forms/C. 2118.

48th Divisional Engineers

2/1st SOUTH MIDLAND FIELD COMPANY R. E.

AUGUST 1 9 1 6

Vol. 15 Sheet 1.

INTELLIGENCE SUMMARY
(Erase heading not required.)

Summaries are contained in F.S. Regs., Part II. and the Staff Manual respectively. Title Pages will be prepared in manuscript.

Place	Date	Hour	Summary of Events and Information	Remarks and references to Appendices
August DOMQUEUR	Aug 3		Dismounted platoon moved to bivouacs at Caesar's Camp near L'Etoile for bivouac	LENS 11 1/100,000
"	8	6 pm	Company moved to LONGVILLERS arriving 7.5 pm	do
LONGVILLERS	9	5.45 am	Moved to AUTHEULE arriving 1 pm	
AUTHEULE	10	5.30 am	Moved to ACHEUX arriving 11.45 am	
SENLIS ACHEUX	13	5.30 am	1 platoon & all transport moved to bivouac near SENLIS, remained 2 sections to bivouacs at AVELUY	
AVELUY	15	5 am	2 sections employed on tram track from X.8.6.67 to join X.3.c.79. 1 section on Brigade HQ dugout at W.12.b.44. 120' of track laid, road cleared, material carried to pits.	
	16	5 am	1200' track carried up - track hurried against towards X.3.c.88.	

Vol 15 Sheet 2.

INTELLIGENCE SUMMARY

(Erase heading not required.)

Summaries are contained in F.S. Regs., Part II. and the Staff Manual respectively. Title Pages will be prepared in manuscript.

Place	Date	Hour	Summary of Events and Information	Remarks and references to Appendices
NEUVE	17	5am	Tram line completed as far as 5th Shed. Work much hampered by shell fire.	
	18	"	190' line laid from 5th Shed towards 19. Brigade HQ dugouts completed. 105' of trench in rear of SKYLINE TRENCH dug 3' deep × 2' wide.	
	19	"	3 sections employed on OVILLERS KEEP. Trenches cleared. Fatigues between X8a74 — X8/s 16 — X 3/s 53. Work continued on Nº 4, 5 & 8 M.G. positions	
	20	"	Mined dugouts were started at X2 C0A, X3a 15, X3 C79, X B6 11, working in 24 hours in 3 × 8 hour shifts. MG emplacements 1 - 5 in OVILLERS KEEP completed	
	21	Aam.	39 gallery cases were fitted, shell fire hampered work considerably [L Matthews] 5 dugouts hung [mounded]	
	22	"	2 reliefs were cancelled by O.R.E. 20 gallery cases & dugout frames erected.	
	23	"	51 gallery cases, 3 dugout frames fitted. Work hampered by shell fire. 1 relief working for 2 hours to clear trench.	

1875 Wt. W593/826 1,000,000 4/15 J.B.C. & A. A.D.S.S./Forms/C. 2118.

INTELLIGENCE SUMMARY

(Erase heading not required.)

Vol 15 Sheet 3

Place	Date	Hour	Summary of Events and Information	Remarks and references to Appendices
MAILLY	24	4am	Work continued in OVILLERS KEEP. No 5 M.G. position complete & trench revetted & fire bays between 95 & 16. 95 gallery cases & dugout frames fitted. Owing to non-arrival of carrying party, ch/15 had to carry up their own frames & cases. Section at SENLIS completed extension & improvement of water supply from ALBERT - BOUZINCOURT area. At the start pumps could only be run for 35 minutes at a time owing to pump going out but on completion of work the pump was run continuously for 1/2 hour. Supply showed no sign of failing.	
"	25	"	65 gallery cases. 3 dugout frames fitted. Make much hampered by shell fire & faulty construction of cases & frames. No to [which was condemned or cored?] to measurements.	
"	26	"	56 gallery cases. 1 dugout frame fitted.	
"	27	6:30 pm	2 sections & transport moved to MAILLY-MAILLET arriving 8 am.	
MAILLY-MAILLET	28	9 am	Remainder of company arrived from AVELUY at	

Vol 15 Sheet 4

INTELLIGENCE SUMMARY
(Erase heading not required.)

Instructions are contained in F. S. Regs., Part II.
and the Staff Manual respectively. Title Pages
will be prepared in manuscript.

Place	Date	Hour	Summary of Events and Information	Remarks and references to Appendices
Mally Maillet St.		Noon	Works in pelotons chiefly clearing Communication trenches & laying boards	
			EXTRACT FROM WEEKLY STATES.	
			STRENGTH. REINFORCEMENTS TRANSFERS KILLED.	
			OFF. OR. OFF. OR. FROM TO. FROM TO. FROM CCS TO.	
	August 5		7 204 2 - 3 - - - - - 1	
"	12		9 214 2 10 - - - - - - -	
"	19		9 209 - - - - - - - - 5	1 officer
"	26		8 207 - 2 - - - - - - 4*	

Shipp
Major
OC 2/1st E. Bn. 2d Co. R.E.

1875 Wt. W593/826 1,000,000 4/15 J.B.C. & A. A.D.S.S./Forms/C. 2118.

48th. DIVISIONAL ENGINEERS

2/1st. S. M. FIELD COY. ROYAL ENGINEERS

SEPTEMBER 1916.

CONFIDENTIAL.

War Diary

-of-

2/1 South Midland Field Company R.E.

From 1-9-16.   To 30-9-16.

(Volume 16)

Army Form C. 2118.

WAR DIARY
or
INTELLIGENCE SUMMARY
(Erase heading not required.)

VOL 16 Sheet 1.

Instructions regarding War Diaries and Intelligence Summaries are contained in F.S. Regs., Part II. and the Staff Manual respectively. Title pages will be prepared in manuscript.

Place	Date	Hour	Summary of Events and Information	Remarks and references to Appendices
MAILLY-MAILLET	Sept 5th		1 section employed in stores near Church at AUCHONVILLERS. 3 sections on BROADWAY, 2nd Avenue & 5th Avenue, cleaning, grading, laying knifeboards. Drains are of permanent nature being made from corrugated iron sheets.	BEAUMONT 57d SE (1+2 parts of) 1/10,000
"	6.	8pm.	Handed over work in right sector - ie WELLINGTON trench - BROADWAY to 225th from 9/6th C. 39th Division.	
"	8		Work continued on 2nd Avenue 7th Avenue on water supply to WHITE CITY & Essex Sr.	
"	9	4pm	Handed over remainder of work in left sector - BROADWAY - WATLING S - to 252 K.P. C. 1030 x of trench boards laid. 920 x corrugated iron drains since taking over.	
"	10	2.30 pm.	Moved to BERTRANCOURT near BUS, arriving 5.15 pm.	
BUS	11	12.20 pm.	Moved to LONGUEVILLETTE via AUTHIE SARTON, arriving 4.45 pm.	
LONGUEVILLETTE	13	2.15 pm.	Moved to HEM, arriving 3pm.	
HEM	14	12.40	Company inspected by General FANSHAWE, CB, Commanding 48th Division.	
"	18	9 am	Moved to METZEROLLES arriving 10.10 a.m.	LENS 11 1/100,000
METZEROLLES	29	9.15 am.	Moved to BERNAVILLE arriving 11.30 a.m.	

1577 Wt. W10791/1773 500,000 1/15 D. D. & L. A.D.S.S./Forms/C. 2118.

Army Form C. 2118.

Vol 16 sheet 2

WAR DIARY
or
INTELLIGENCE SUMMARY.
(Erase heading not required.)

Place	Date	Hour	Summary of Events and Information	Remarks and references to Appendices
BERNAVILLE Now at Bernaville	29	8·30 am	Moved to SVS St Leger via Frevillers, Le Souich.	
			EXTRACT FROM WEEKLY STATES.	

DATE	STRENGTH		REINFORCEMENTS			TRANSFERS		KILLED	CCS.	
	OFF	OR	OFF	OR	FROM		TO		FROM	TO
Sept 2nd	9×	217	—	10	—		—	—	—	—
9th	10×	217	1	—	—		—	—	—	—
16th	10×	216	—	—	—		—	—	—	1
23rd	10×	218⊙	—	5	—		—	—	—	—
30th	10×	223	—	6	—		1	1	—	—

× 1 attached Corps HQ.

⊙ 1 man struck off strength but 1 extra on base.

[Signature] Major
O.C. 2/1st B.M. FIELD Coy., R.E.
Date 1–10–16
48th DIVISION

Vol 17

War Diary

of

2/1st South Midland Field Co. R.E. (T.)

From 1st Octr 1916 to 31st Octr 1916.

(Volume 17)
5 sheets

Army Form C. 2118.

WAR DIARY
of
INTELLIGENCE SUMMARY.
(Erase heading not required.)

Instructions regarding War Diaries and Intelligence Summaries are contained in F. S. Regs., Part II. and the Staff Manual respectively. Title pages will be prepared in manuscript.

Vol 17 sheet 1.

Place	Date	Hour	Summary of Events and Information	Remarks and references to Appendices
Sos. St. Leger	Oct 1	10:30 a.m.	Moved to Halloy, arriving 3pm.	Lens 11 1/100,000
Halloy	3	10:45 a.m.	Moved to Grenas, arriving 11:30 am.	
Grenas	4	9:30 am	HQ & 2 sections moved to Souastre, arriving 3:30 pm.	
Souastre	5		Part of No 4 Section employed in stores, remainder of Company working on Thorpe St, more communication trenches to front line & through tramways. Offs for Signals.	
"	7		L/t Brigade Division were started. "Dugout for KA" off Thorpe St. In addition to above work, a tunnel was started from Tunnel St. to connect up with 2 tunnels dug by Tunnelling Co. (Lat. Moisenay). Tunnel St. itself was an old trench was carefully cleaned with hidden so as to shew no trace of occupation.	
"	8		6 small Signal shelters were erected, 1 in front line Sd YUZ, 1 in YUZ H in Eblie. Ladders were placed in front & second lines & steps made on firing steps in support line.	
"	9		First second line was buttonholed. 2 Companies 5th Sussex completed buttonholing 6th Menin, Mills St. Kellerman. Trench tramline from RE stores to South Barrier repaired made good. Branch RE tramps at Eblie, Calvaire, Tunnel St. prepared.	
"	10		Tramline laid from South Barrier to junction of Third St. Tunnel St. Signal Off Brigade HQ completed. Site of Emplacement of abutter seen are started in last trenches New St.	

Army Form C. 2118.

Vol 17 Sheet 2.

WAR DIARY
or
INTELLIGENCE SUMMARY.
(Erase heading not required.)

Place	Date	Hour	Summary of Events and Information	Remarks and references to Appendices
SOUASTRE	10		Recesses for rations made in parapet in THORP ST & roofed. 40' of access to FONQUEVILLERS - SOUASTRE ROAD erected.	
"	11		Notice boards fixed at junction of all trenches, also quantity of OP down boards. Tram lines prepared from junction THORP ST & TUNNEL ST to advanced RE Dumps in TUNNEL ST. It was not proposed to lay this track until the last possible moment. large quantities of all RE stores were carried up to dumps & made up into man loads.	
"	12.		Work started on following mined dugouts. OPs. For 241 Brig RFA in YIDDISH ST: 240 & 243 in R line E of YANKEE ST: 240 - 241 in R line at same place; 242 in R line E of HADDON 4m 241 in WOMAN ST. TUNNEL ST was completed, being deepened & muchboarded.	
"	13		Excavations for all OPs were completed frames carried up. Tunnel from TUNNEL ST to MOUSETRAP completed except for timbering last 5'. Work was delayed owing to 5.9 HV shell piercing the roof. Damage to tunnel was small but 1 NCO working in tunnel was killed by direct hit.	

1577 Wt. W.10791/1773 500,000 1/15 D. D. & L. A.D.S.S./Forms/C. 2118.

Army Form C. 2118.

VOL 17 Sheet 3

WAR DIARY
or
INTELLIGENCE SUMMARY.
(Erase heading not required.)

Place	Date	Hour	Summary of Events and Information	Remarks and references to Appendices
SOUASTRE	14		Dugout for 242 Bing RFA & Thorp St fitted with bunking layer & bags. Completed except for small details. eg. Chairs. Lake etc. Transcribed for OPs in R line erected & rails for roof carried up. Advanced RE dumps completed with full stocks of hole materials.	
"	15		OP for 240 & 243 Brig. completed & entrances started & to Dugout. 350' tram track from LA HAIE - BLUFF repaired & trams made from FONQUEVILLERS - THORP St repaired where damaged by shell fire. Heavy T.M. emplacement near Church FONQUEVILLERS started. Tunnel from TUNNEL St to MOUSETRAP finally completed with intermediate cross.	
"	16		OP in WOMAN St completed.	
"	19		YIDDISH St OP completed. Both OPs in R line E of YANKEE complete & 21' ft of gallery completed on both. OP in R line E of HADDON partly erected & 24' ft of gallery completed. 25' gallery for OP in WOMAN St completed. T.M. emplacement completed. Handed over work to 2/1 West Riding F.C. Noted to MARLINCOURT arriving 1 pm.	LENS !! 1/100,000
"	20		Mounted Section moved to TAMAS via DOULLENS arriving 6.30pm.	
MARLINCOURT	24		Mounted Section moved to BRESLE arriving 4pm. Dismounted section moved from	
"	25		WALLINCOURT to BRESLE by motor lorries arriving 5.30pm.	

Army Form C. 2118.

Vol 17 Sheet 4.

WAR DIARY
or
INTELLIGENCE SUMMARY.
(Erase heading not required.)

Place	Date	Hour	Summary of Events and Information	Remarks and references to Appendices
BRESLE.	26		March to MAMETZ WOOD with all transport. Roads beyond CONTALMAISON impassable to wheeled traffic. Billets for company now erected. Most of transport stuck in the mud over 1½ miles of road: eventually got some huts for the men on fringe of a lake for the horse lines. It was mutually decided that the latter end of October was not altogether the best period of the year in which to picnic.	
MAMETZ WOOD	27		Whole company — less details employed in erecting available huts + bivouacs — clearing refuse from road — employed on CONTALMAISON — LONGUEVAL Road from BEAVER Road to BAZENTIN CROSS. Work prevented hundreds by continuous traffic — scarcity of material.	
"	30		Work continued on road; weather conditions all against progress, continuous rain + traffic necessitating the work being done afresh every day	
"	31		"Do"	

1577 Wt.W10791/1773 500,000 1/15 D. D. & L. A.D.S.S./Forms/C. 2118.

Army Form C. 2118.

Vol 17 Sheet 5

WAR DIARY
or
INTELLIGENCE SUMMARY.
(Erase heading not required.)

Instructions regarding War Diaries and Intelligence Summaries are contained in F.S. Regs., Part II and the Staff Manual respectively. Title pages will be prepared in manuscript.

Place	Date	Hour	Summary of Events and Information	Remarks and references to Appendices

EXTRACT FROM WEEKLY STATES.

DATE.	STRENGTH.		REINFORCEMENTS		TRANSFERS		KILLED			Remarks
	OFF	OR.	OFF	OR.	FROM	TO	FROM	TO		
Oct 7	10ˣ	224	-	-	-	1	-	-		x 1 attached VIII Corps HQ.
" 14	10ˣ	225	-	2	-	-	-	1		
" 21	10ˣ	221	-	-	1	1	3	1		
" 28	10ˣ	221	-	-	-	-	-	-		

O.C. [signature]
9/18th B.M. FIELD Coy., R.E.
No. 31-10-16
48th DIVISION

[signature] Major

CONFIDENTIAL

War Diary

of

2/1st South Midland Field Company
Royal Engineers

From 1st Nov 1916 To 30th Nov 1916.

(Volume 18)

WAR DIARY
or
INTELLIGENCE SUMMARY.
(Erase heading not required.)

Army Form C. 2118.

VOL. 18. sheet 1.

Place	Date	Hour	Summary of Events and Information	Remarks and references to Appendices
MAMETZ WOOD.	1916 Nov 3		Work continued on CONTALMAISON - LONGUEVAL Road. X 17b 72 (57°SE) - S14b 99 (57°SW) About 110 pioneers 1680 infantry parties were employed, cleaning mud from surface, levelling & filling in shell holes and unloading stone etc.	57 D SE Edition 2.D 1/20,000 and 57 D SW Edition 4.A 1/20,000
"	7		2300 x of road completed, an average of about 200x per day varying as materials & helpers etc were available also according to the amount of transport on actually using the road. During this period the company received a letter from CE III Corps expressing his keen appreciation of the progress made under very trying conditions	
"	10		2612 x of road finished for traffic up to BAZENTIN CROSS. Moved from old camp taken occupied by 74th Field Coys.	S14b 9592 57 D SW.
"	15		Infantry parties here gradually decreasing in numbers, an average day being about 4 F.S. & 100 pioneers. Work on road chiefly rettening digging drains at sides, placing and ramping loads of stone on soft road portion. Corps Commander specially ordered that company should not return Division but should remain on the road until completed	

1577 Wt. W10791/1773 500,000 1/15 D. D. & L. A.D.S.S./Forms/C. 2118.

Army Form C. 2118.

Vol 15 sheet 2

WAR DIARY
or
INTELLIGENCE SUMMARY.
(Erase heading not required.)

Place	Date	Hour	Summary of Events and Information	Remarks and references to Appendices
MAMETZ WOOD	Nov. 20		Work progressing on road. 400× sleeper ties had been laid. Orders for unloading of road material ammunition.	
	25		Construction of road no longer favorably reported on by Engineer in Chief. 1 section moved to MARTINPUICH to assist a section of 91st Field Co. CE II Corps again expressed his satisfaction at progress of work through GOC 48th Division. 1 sec. 91st Fd. C. R.E. attached for work on road. 300 yards of pit prop & sleeper roadway average width 18' with turning point 36' × 36' at end laid on N. side of stone siding BAZENTIN station to serve as R.E. dump for 1st Division. 100* of platform revetted for unloading stores.	
	26	5.30 p.	Captain Crawford proceeded on leave to ENGLAND.	
	30		Work entered on road. Curb & stone edging practically completed. Work concentrated on permanent drainage.	

1577 Wt. W10791/1773 500,000 1/15 D. D. & L. A.D.S.S./Forms/C. 2118.

Army Form C. 2118.

WAR DIARY
or
INTELLIGENCE SUMMARY.
(Erase heading not required.)

Place	Date	Hour	Summary of Events and Information	Remarks and references to Appendices
	DATE 1916		EXTRACT from WEEKLY STATES.	

	STRENGTH		REINFORCEMENTS		TRANSFERS		KILLED		C.C.S.	
	OFF.	O.R.	OFF.	O.R.	FROM	TO			FROM	TO
Nov. 4	10 ˣ	224	—	4	—	—	—	—	—	—
11	10 *	224	—	—	—	—	—	—	—	—
18	10 ⊙	221	—	—	—	—	—	—	—	—
25	10	222	—	1	—	1⊗	—	—	—	4

Actual strength on Nov. 26th
7   210

DETACHED
XIV Corps   1
III Corps   1
Hospital   1
Leave   —
H.Q. R.E. 48th Div   3
48th Div School   1
Inoculation   2
Div. Train   1
Hospital   3
Leave   —
                 ——
              3 12

Remarks:
×1 Attached XIV Corps
* 1 ICE Fcd to Hospital
⊙ 1 Lt. Currit wound from Hospital
⊙ H.Q. Currit attached III Corps H.Q.
⊗ No 38.10 Sapper S.C. Emmet from 1st F.S. Dn Co.

[signature] Major
O.C. 2/1st Dn. Co. R.E.

CONFIDENTIAL

War Diary

of

2/1st South Midland Field Co.

Royal Engineers.

From 1st Dec. 1916 to 31st Dec. 1916

(Volume 19)

Army Form C. 2118.

Vol — sheet 1

WAR DIARY
or
INTELLIGENCE SUMMARY.
(Erase heading not required.)

Place	Date	Hour	Summary of Events and Information	Remarks and references to Appendices
MAMETZ WOOD S.13.C.33	1916 Dec 1		Work continued on Contalmaison — Bazentin Circus road. Banks on each side of road cut back 9' clear & edge of road & side drains dug. Average of 350 infantry employed daily including party of 60 detailed for unloading trucks of road material & loading into wagons.	
	Dec 7		No.4 Section relieved No 3 section at MARTINPUICH	
		10 am	MAJOR BRIGGS proceeded on leave to ENGLAND	
	11		D. Cresswell took over company.	
	12		Construction of sleeper road between BAZENTIN STATION coor & BEAVER ROAD commenced.	
	14		2nd Lt Sutton returned to Coy HQrs from MARTINPUICH. Work continued on CONTALMAISON – BAZENTIN CIRCUS Road as for Dec 1. Weekly Med member of infantry has been reduced to average 120.	
	15		No.4 moved to BOTTOM WOOD to take over putting scheme at X 29 b 68.	
	19.		Work on road handed over to A Co Labur Battr. During the time the Company has on this road, 2600 x were made available	

1577 Wt.W10791/1773 500,000 1/15 D.D.&L. A.D.S.S./Forms/C. 2118.

Army Form C. 2118.

Vol 19 sheet #2

WAR DIARY
or
INTELLIGENCE SUMMARY.
(Erase heading not required)

Place	Date	Hour	Summary of Events and Information	Remarks and references to Appendices
MAMETZ WOOD S128 33	DEC 19.		For all conditions of traffic over a width of 24 ft, where previously pack animals had the greatest difficulty in getting even light loads along its length. Some idea of the amount of work put in on this section can be gathered from the following figures, dating from Oct 27th to Dec 19th.	
			WAGONS. LOADS STONE. LOGS. SLEEPERS. 1399. 5697. 9588. 4639.	
	25.		No work for the day. Turkeys + xmas plum pudding beer spirits for dinner.	
	30		44 Nissen huts erected at Bottom Wood. Complete with stoves. Our 9.0"Long between Grave Dramville have started at S 10 c. Beaver Road are progressing slowly may to take off .... Aeroplane alighting ground at X 11 a started. Group amplet a series of shell holes which have to be filled up with old sandbags from former batty. Empl. cemento. Quantity of men shell holes near Infroson spring proceeding.	

Army Form C. 2118.

Vol 19 Sheet 5

WAR DIARY
or
INTELLIGENCE SUMMARY.
(Erase heading not required.)

Instructions regarding War Diaries and Intelligence Summaries are contained in F. S. Regs., Part II. and the Staff Manual respectively. Title pages will be prepared in manuscript.

Place	Date	Hour	Summary of Events and Information	Remarks and references to Appendices

EXTRACT FROM WEEKLY RETURN.

DATE	STRENGTH OFF	STRENGTH OR	REINFORCEMENTS OFF	REINFORCEMENTS OR	TRANSFERS FROM	TRANSFERS TO	KILLED	CCS FROM	CCS TO	Remarks
Dec 2	10ˣ	224	-	3	1⊙	1	-	-	-	⊙ 975 Spr Brittman to ½ Fd Co
9	10ˣ	223	-	-	-	-	-	-	-	
15	10ˣ	220	-	1	4⊕	-	-	-	-	⊕ G.R.O. 1693
23	10ˣ	219	-	1	-	-	-	-	1	ˣ includes 5 attached
30	10ˣ	224	-	5	-	-	-	-	-	

Actual strength on Dec 30.

OFF	OR
7	211

Detached.
Off. OR.
Cp.   -   3
XII   -   3
Leave - 2
Bn Hq R.E. - 1
" Train 1 —
" School of Instruction — 2
A.D.S.S./Forms/C. 2118. School of Northern —
Sick Hospital 3 13

M.W. Crawford Capt.
for OC 2/1 NM Fd Co RE

Vol 20

CONFIDENTIAL.

WAR DIARY

of

2/1st. (South Midland) Field Company, R.E.

From 1st January 1917..........to........31st January 1917.

Army Form C. 2118.

WAR DIARY
or
INTELLIGENCE SUMMARY.
(Erase heading not required.)

VOL 20 Sheet 1.

Instructions regarding War Diaries and Intelligence Summaries are contained in F. S. Regs., Part II and the Staff Manual respectively. Title pages will be prepared in manuscript.

Place	Date	Hour	Summary of Events and Information	Remarks and references to Appendices
MAMETZ WOOD S13 b 33.	4	7 AM.	Cour at S.10.c. completed to time. Owing to absence of sleepers the pit could not be made really satisfactory, as the 3" boarding supplied had rough edges. Consequently gaps were left whilst flooring.	TRENCH MAP 57d SE .2.D 1/20.000.
	5		Cour from BEAVER ROAD to BAYERNN Station now completed. The Company ceased working for III Corps were attached to 50th Division on mile line with the exception of Camp at BOTTOM WOOD which had to be completed. Progress on this camp at the time was slow owing to non-arrival of stores from Quempil. Work on aeroplane alighting ground at X 11a was not proceeded with owing to [illegible] orders of [?] 50th Div. Work was started on extension of [?] tramline from M.23.c.75 to HEXHAM ROAD also on Cruciform post at S.29.b.95.45. This work was in bad condition & trees of branches fallen on owing to setting frames being spaced too wide. All work was to be done by night	57c S.W Edition 4 1/20.000.
	6		Tramline to HEXHAM ROAD repaired & completed. Work on this continues. Tram line from FORKS ROAD Junction M.30.c.96 to JACOB'S CORNER commenced. Poling boards for walking way & sleepers under the tracks being the principal work.	
	11			

1577 Wt. W10791/1773 500,000 1/15 D. D. & L. A.D.S.S./Forms/C. 2118.

Army Form C. 2118.

Vol 20 Sheet 2

WAR DIARY
or
INTELLIGENCE SUMMARY
(Erase heading not required.)

Place	Date	Hour	Summary of Events and Information	Remarks and references to Appendices
MAMETZ WOOD S13b33	July 16		Work continued on Post 16. Parties with carrying parties from 50th Div & dense bush interfered with progress. My materials. Tanko road – tadray Conser Myn line progressed quite satisfactorily. Post however making the job of taking up sleepers making a really satisfactory formation, somewhat arduous.	TRENCH MAP 57D SE 2D 1/20,000
	18.		Major Briggs returns from leave. Heanrel Command. In addition to other jobs in hand, a mile post was commenced at railhead at Hexham Road to allow inter parties from Crek's Dump take parted sured into Sweeney tanks	
	21		Steven continued. Posts make progress on Post 15 & hauling to Patrick Catoutil Kny Islam. Grand Mot 20 has for a supply of 2' Rut is now a continuous occurence for fake tote between on Rd to call upon in hand.	
	26		All goods with area was handed over to Rd Fr G Anzac Corps.	
	27		Section worn to CAPPY for hutting. HQ one main 2 sections moved by road to CERISEY arriving 11.0pm	

1577 Wt. W10791/1773 500,000 1/15 D. D. & L. A.D.S.S./Forms/C. 2118.

Army Form C. 2118.

Vol 20 sheet 3

WAR DIARY
or
INTELLIGENCE SUMMARY.
(Erase heading not required.)

Instructions regarding War Diaries and Intelligence Summaries are contained in F. S. Regs., Part II. and the Staff Manual respectively. Title pages will be prepared in manuscript.

Place	Date	Hour	Summary of Events and Information	Remarks and references to Appendices
CERISY	30.			FRANCE AMIENS 17 1/100.000
	6/1/17		Major Briggs left to join GHQ School of Instruction at LE POLCG	to U.K. to take up Commission
			Extract from Weekly States	
			STRENGTH REINFORCEMENTS TRANSFERS KILLED	
			OFF. OR. OFF OR FROM TO FROM TO	
			10 224 - - - - - -	
	13.		10 223 - 2 - - - 1	
	20		10 221 1 - - 4/+ - 1	2
	21		10 220 - - - + - -	2
			Actual strength at 31/1/17. Detached	
			OFF OR OFF OR. OFF. OR.	
			4 20D XIV Corps 1 Hospital 1 1	
			III Corps 1 III Corps Camp	
			48 Bn School 1 GHQ 3 10	
			Div MGLE 3 School 1 2 20	
			in Train 2 3 6	

Vol 21.

Confidential

War Diary of 477
(South Midland) Field
Coy. R.E. from February
1st to February 28th 1917.

Volume 21.

Army Form C. 2118.

WAR DIARY
or
INTELLIGENCE SUMMARY.
(Erase heading not required.)

Vol 21 Sheet 1

Place	Date	Hour	Summary of Events and Information	Remarks and references to Appendices
CERISEY	FEB. 1	7.40 am	Moved to FRISE.	6 c.m.m 2yds
FRISE	3.	6 pm	2 sections moved into line, billets at H36.c.33, took over from 757 Co of French Engineers. Trenches generally were in very good condition but nearly all fall directly the thaw came.	
	6.		Efforts of 2 sections chiefly engaged in forming a company store outside billets in clearing up collecting fragments of trench stores which were lying all over the area. A dump in 10gpv was complete. Ammunition to left battalion HQ - company HQ in CHAMINADE started.	
	10		New dressing station at junction of GUILBERT ROMAN DESFOSSES was started. 2 new entrances were proposed. Mica 3rd Emergency exit in STETTIN Well in SUCRERIE at FLAUCOURT was cleared of debris, but pumps etc demolised were under 3½' of water. This matter was left over for a time. Preparations made to erect a shelter after in well off ROMAN DESFOSSES.	
	12.		During a heavy bombardment on 5th previous to hostile raid, large pieces of frozen earth had fallen & blocked various trenches. Attempts were made to clear these with guncotton - were not particularly successful	

Army Form C. 2118.

VOL 21 Sheet 2

WAR DIARY
or
INTELLIGENCE SUMMARY.
(Erase heading not required.)

Place	Date	Hour	Summary of Events and Information	Remarks and references to Appendices
FRISE	12.		Our tress in front of our line in CHASSEUR were prepared for demolition but owing to intense cold, the cement made a packing for the charge fuse, & no canon slight air space which failed to bring down the trees. The other no canon was successful.	
	14		Major E. BRIGGS returned from GHQ. Retched of instruction & passed command.	
BOIS VERT	17	3pm	HQ's & section at FRISE moved to new HQ's at BOIS VERT G.36.b.84.	
	19		No. 4 section (relieved No. 1 section & continued front line work. No. 3 section rejoined the Co. from CAPPY where the, had been employed in hutting (HQ Bn. HQ)	
	20		No. 3 section relieved No. 2 section & continued front line work. Front line work consisted of OP's for RFA, improving & repairing existing dug out accommodation, widening road at RE dump, water supply in DESIRÉ VALLEY. work of 2 sections in back area comprised road upkeep & repairs from STD to HERBECOURT. HERBS. to FLAUCOURT. FLAUCOURT - BIACHES. up to forward RE dump.	

Army Form C. 2118.

Vol 21 sheet 3

WAR DIARY
or
INTELLIGENCE SUMMARY.
(Erase heading not required.)

Place	Date	Hour	Summary of Events and Information	Remarks and references to Appendices
BOISVERT	1917 Feb 18		Thaw set in severely & all trenches soon became impassable. Large flakes & flecks of earth falling into them.	
	27		Large working parties supplied by Bde in reserve. 580 men for clearing communication trenches ACHILLE, BEAUSEJOUR & ROMAIN DESPOSIS forward of DESIRÉ VALLEY. Very little progress made however owing to heavy state of the ground & fatigue of the working parties who had a 5 mile march up to the work & the same back. Work as above continued.	
	28		Rear sections working on road repairs with inf. parties of 140 daily, water supply at HERISE COURT & improving the accomodation at Point 572 by providing an ablution & hand foot bath shed & 2 drying rooms.	

Army Form C. 2118.

vol. 21 sheet 4

WAR DIARY
or
INTELLIGENCE SUMMARY.
(Erase heading not required.)

Place	Date	Hour	Summary of Events and Information	Remarks and references to Appendices
	1917. Feb. 3		Extract from WEEKLY STATES	
			STRENGTH — OFF. O.R. — 10 220	
			REINFORCEMENTS — OFF. O.R. — 1 1	
	10		10 219 — — 1 — 1	
	17		10 218 — 1 1 — 1	x Sapper Ball WF to Rnfts. found.
	24		10 221 1 3 — 1 1 —	
	Feb 24		Actual strength OFF. 8 O.R. 207	
			Attached OFF. O.R.	
			XIV Corps 1 1	
			III Corps — 1	
			Hq RE 48th Div — 3	
			Div Train — 2	
			48th Div. School 1 —	
			Leave — 2	
			Hospital — 4	
			2 14	

Whyte Major

O.C. 477 (8m.) Tel Co R.E.

<u>CONFIDENTIAL</u>

<u>War Diary</u>

- of -

<u>477ᵗʰ S.M. Field Co. R.E.</u>

<u>From 1ˢᵗ March 1917. To 31ˢᵗ March 1917.</u>

(Volume <u>22</u>)
<u>6 sheets</u>

Vol 22

WAR DIARY
or
INTELLIGENCE SUMMARY.
(Erase heading not required.)

Army Form C. 2118.

Vol Sheet 22 sheet 1

Place	Date	Hour	Summary of Events and Information	Remarks and references to Appendices
BOISVERT	MARCH			Ref G2 G 1/407000
	1		2 sections employed in DESIRÉ VALLEY. Work continued on O.P.'s, water supply and general trench work.	
	7		2 sections at BOISVERT engaged on hutting and road repairs.	
	10.		No 1 section relieved No 3 section in forward area. Work resumed on lining 2nd line in front of HERING COURT, thaw having set in	
	12		No 2 section relieved No 4 section in forward area.	
	16/17		4 sappers from No 3 section assisted in raid on LA MAISONETTE Coppice. Charge of explosives for destroying dugouts etc. German lines found to be unoccupied except for about 12 Grenadiers who were captured. O.O. 1+2 lines held by raiding parts of 4th O+B + 5th Glos. Included hole blown 5 hr. Work completed up to how hand 17h. supply at HERING COURT, 3 O.P.'s for R.A. PLUGSCOURT, BIACHES ROAD, water supply at HERING COURT, dug outs for B.H. in CATHERIMADÉ, OBSERVATOIRE + ETERPIGNY trenches, dug outs for B. Hq's in IGLAU, dying shed at point 512, trench foot treatment shed for 60 persons at HERING COURT, Gum boot drying room for 60 pairs tn at HERING COURT	

Army Form C. 2118.

WAR DIARY
or
INTELLIGENCE SUMMARY.
(Erase heading not required.)

WE 22 sheet 2

Place	Date	Hour	Summary of Events and Information	Remarks and references to Appendices
BOISVERT FARM	1917 17		Belt with lifting gear at H.35.d.53. (DESIRÉ VALLEY) supplying 800 galls. per hour, beside village of trenches, road repair etc. The enemy having retired E. of the SOMME area previously held by them was reconnoitred & arrangements made for repairs to roads, bridges etc.	Ref 62c / 1/40,000
	18			
GARDEN FARM 0.8.d.75.	19	6 am	Company moved to GARDEN FARM and started work on reconstruction of bridge at LAHUIRE FARM, and footbridges across SOMME canal & marshes between LAHUIRE FARM & LA CHAPELLETTE ① at 0.3.d.42. ② at 0.3.d.75. Road cleared of rubble & trenches filled thro' BRETIEUX.	
DOINGT	21 (6.30)		Company & all transport moved to DOINGT. Work started at 7-30 am on ① Road repairs - large craters in road at 0.12.c.70 and P.8.a.54 ② Bridges across COLOGNE near at DOINGT. 2 sections joined "WARD'S" mobile advanced column and started work on road craters at J.31.c.87 and bridge across COLOGNE River at J.33.c.25.	
	22		Work continued on above road craters & also one at 0.6.a.39 & DOINGT bridge.	

WAR DIARY
or
INTELLIGENCE SUMMARY

Army Form C. 2118.

vol 2 — sheet 3.

Place	Date	Hour	Summary of Events and Information	Remarks and references to Appendices
DOINGT	1917 Mar 23		Work continued on craters at P.8.a.5↑ & O.6.a.39.	Ref 62 c / 40,000
	" 24		Bridges at DOINGT finished to take 3 ton lorries ie 5 tons on axle. Advanced hostile actions completed bridge at J.33.c.25 and another at TINCOURT J.24.a.9, both to take inf. in fours, field guns. Work continued on craters at P.8.a.5↑ & O.6.a.39.	
	" 25		Bridge at J.33.c.25 remodelled to take 3 ton lorries. Road cleared of "splint" at J.33.c. Road deviation at J.31.a.40. improved, and work continued at O.6.a.39.	
	" 26	11am	Watches advanced 1 hour to 12 midnight. Lewis slept last. Road thro' crate O.6.a.39 completed for heavy traffic. Work started on craters at J.24.d.62 & J.21.a.78. & road cleared of O.8. Fd.A.	
	" 27		Road work continued. Bridge at MARQUAIX K.2.o.6.3.8. Completed. Work started on bridges at BUIRE.	
TINCOURT	" 28		Hq's Nos 1 3 & 4 sections moved to TINCOURT. No 2 section remaining at DOINGT to complete bridges to take 17 tons on one axle. Hq's in HAMEL J.24.6.99	

WAR DIARY or INTELLIGENCE SUMMARY

Army Form C. 2118.

Vol 22 sheet 4.

Place	Date	Hour	Summary of Events and Information	Remarks and references to Appendices
HAMEL	1917 Mar 29		Bridges at BOIRE Completed, road clearance made to bridge at CHERISY bridge at CHERISY further strengthened. Work continued on DOINGT bridge, unexpected difficulties in holding abutments owing to loose nature of ground. Shelter to K.plan.	Ref. 62c. 1/40,000
	.30		All transport moved up to HAMEL.	
	.31		DOINGT bridge Completed for 17 tons in 1 mile at 7-30 p.m. HARGUVAL - VILLERS-FAUCON road repaired & drainage holes made, crater at E.2.a.5.3.	
			During the period Mar 18-31 our first experience of the warfare, which mainly consisted of road repairs, all important cross roads having been mined, the craters ranging from 15' to 50' deep & 20' to 80' diameter. Road bridges across COLOGNE river all of which were demolished. In all 7 of these were completed, average span 24'. All material was found near site. Water supply. — the river COLOGNE being the main source of supply, it's a few wells were cleaned out & windlasses fitted. Searching for mines in the few houses left standing & various derelicts, mess, guns, traps.	

1577 Wt. W10791/1773 500,000 1/15 D. D. & L. A.D.S.S./Forms/C. 2118.

Army Form C. 2118.

Vol. 22 sheet 5.

WAR DIARY
or
INTELLIGENCE SUMMARY.
(Erase heading not required.)

Place	Date	Hour	Summary of Events and Information	Remarks and references to Appendices
	1917.		Stores & other devices laid by the enemy. Avery ingenious electro-chemical delaying device was discovered with a 100 lb charge of H.E. in cellar of house occupied by 1/4/5 Inf. Bde. The necessity of utilising large infantry working parties for the repair of roads strengthened the desirability of permanently attaching to Div. G. at least 100 inf. If this were done a personnel party of 100 men would do as much work as the daily changing parties of 400/500 often obtain with much difficulty, & frequently having to march 6 or 7 miles to the site of work. Much unnecessary correspondence & organisation work would also be saved & it would lend troops promoting a better feeling between the R.E. & Infantry, the former having invariably to shoulder the blame for any miss takes made by the various & too numerous units this which a requisition for a single working party at present passes	

WAR DIARY
or
INTELLIGENCE SUMMARY.
(Erase heading not required.)

Army Form C. 2118.

vol 22 sheet 6

Extract from WEEKLY STATES.

Place	Date	Hour	STRENGTH		REINFORCEMENTS		TRANSFERS		KILLED		CAS.		Remarks and references to Appendices
			OFF.	O.R.	OFF.	O.R.	FROM	TO			FROM	TO	
	1917												
	Mar 3		9	220				1*				1	*Lt Byrd to England (sick)
	10		9	219		2						3	
	17		9	219			1						
	24		9	220			1						
	31		9	216								5	

Actual Strength
OFF / O.R.
9 / 205

Mar 31

Attached
	OFF	O.R.
XIV Corps		1
125 Inf Bde	1	3
464 Fd Coy RE		2
Div from R.E. Stores		3
Hospital		
	2	11

D Whipp Major
O.C. 477 2nd Co R.E.

CONFIDENTIAL.

War Diary

— of —

477th South Midland Field Company.

Royal Engineers.

From 1st April 1917 To 30th April 1917

(Volume 23.)
No. of sheets 10.

Vol 23

WAR DIARY
or
INTELLIGENCE SUMMARY.
(Erase heading not required.)

Army Form C. 2118.

Vol 23 Sheet 1

Place	Date	Hour	Summary of Events and Information	Remarks and references to Appendices
TINCOURT	APRIL			
	1.		Reconnaissance of roads, wells etc in EMILIE & EPEHY made. Filling in of craters at railway crossings in E 23 d at the cross roads BEAUSEJOUR - E30 b c started.	62c/40.000
	3		Two out of the three craters in E 23 c completed for horse transport. Repairs to various entrances in VILLERS FAUCON - SAULCOURT road started, also repairs to various damaged wells in VILLERS started. Well in SUCRERIE at St EMILIE was partially cleared of débris, broken machinery etc.	
	5		All craters in E 23 c completed. Surface made good. Road from St EMILIE to RONSSOY & EPEHY reconnoitred. Search made for alleged mine under Hospice Crypts in EPEHY but nothing found. Owing to all the cellars being blown in, any indications of mining has been very thoroughly hidden.	
	7		Some mining point near mill at E 23 c 07 in VILLERS FAUCON started. Shaft water after sunk on site. Increased accommodation made for baths in TINCOURT. Water found for carts started at J 24 a 22.	
	9		Water point in TINCOURT continued. Much work being carried round spring to keep out surface water. Wells in VILLERS - FAUCON - RONSSOY were worked on. A large quantity of mud, débris, wild machinery removed. Bridge at J 24 a 91 made suitable for lorry traffic.	

WAR DIARY
INTELLIGENCE SUMMARY

Army Form C. 2118.

Vol 23 Sheet 2.

Place	Date	Hour	Summary of Events and Information	Remarks and references to Appendices
TINCOURT	APRIL 10		Resting. Kit inspection. Coy baths and reissue with clean clothing during day.	
	12		Work on water front at TINCOURT contd and offwire talks contd at same place. Work on cleaning wells in VILLERS FAUCON & ROISEL contd. 126' run of trench tramway mad in DIV. RE Store TINCOURT for civilian in adverned areas.	
	13.		Work unproving and increasing billetting accommodation in VILLERS FAUCON & LONGAVESNES commenced. Nos 1 & 3 Sects engaged on this. Sects 1 & 4 being engaged on "back" work. Subsidence of ramp on new 5' ton lorry bridge at CARTIGNY due to settling of "made" ground repaired by laying addl sets grouted with cement for 6' on each end of bridge.	
			Additional accommodation made for 70 men at VILLERS FAUCON and for 66 men at LONGAVESNES. Further 84' of trench tramway made at DIV. RE site. Work on spring and offwire talks at TINCOURT contd. Manyeuvres well Ho' high demolished in BUIRE.	
	14		Accommodation provided for 12/26 men (247 total) at VILLER FAUCON and 50 men (116 total) at LONGAVESNES. Work on spring and offwire talks at TINCOURT contd	
	15		Accommodation provided for 25 men (107 total) at VILLER FAUCON and 10 men (126 total) at LONGAVESNES. 50% of concrete work completed. 2,400 gal tanks erected on chargings tripod line land and filtings connected at TINCOURT spring. Progress made with offwire talks.	
	16		Accommodation for 50 men (157 total) mode at VILLER FAUCON and for 84 men (210 total) at LONGAVESNES	

WAR DIARY
or
INTELLIGENCE SUMMARY.
(Erase heading not required.)

Army Form C. 2118.

VOL 23 Sh 3

Place	Date	Hour	Summary of Events and Information	Remarks and references to Appendices
TINCOURT 46 (central)	APRIL 16 (contd)		Work on TINCOURT Siding — L & F. hand-filled console work 75% complete	
	17		Accommodation made for 15 men (172 hours) at VILLER FAUCON. TINCOURT Siding console work completed. BLUE LINE of DEFENCE ammunition and plan sent to CRE. Following table of feeds for complying horses sent into force today.	

CLASS		NO	FEED	TOTAL	REMARKS
H.D		16	18	288	These feeds are ONLY for horses actually at work during the day at work. 1lb is to be deducted for each horse not at work and given to poor horses. MULES excepted.
L.D		27	13	351	
Riders	over 15	10	13	130	
	under 15	9	10	90	
MULES		18	6	108	

| | 18 | | Work as for 17th proceeded with until noon when billets were reserved for all available men to proceed to K.11.c & K.11.b. (Sh 62c 1st Ed 20,000) and erect new camps for (a) DIV HQ and (b) RA & RE HQ. This scheme was made of several epidiorms of camp annex (delay action) rather accentuated. Sub 1,2 & 3 undertook this work and in half day partly erected 3 NISSEN huts and 2. 28'x16" (AMIENS type) huts. Wagons and GS transport remained at TINCOURT. Also debates to H Sect. | |

1577 Wt. W10791/1773 500,000 1/15 D. D. & L. A.D.S.S./Forms/C. 2118.

WAR DIARY
INTELLIGENCE SUMMARY.
(Erase heading not required.)

Army Form C. 2118.

VOL 23 SH 4.

Place	Date	Hour	Summary of Events and Information	Remarks and references to Appendices
Nr ROSEL K.11.a. K.11.b.	19.		Construction of new camps cont'd. 2 NISSEN huts complete and 1 NISSEN u. 4 AMIENS huts under construction. 1 ARMSTRONG hut erected (R.A. camp). Also necessary latrines, urinoirs, washhouses, under construction.	
	20.		Construction of new camps cont'd. 1 NISSEN hut completed (3 hours) also 4 AMIENS huts completed. 2 further AMIENS huts under construction. Also additional outhouses latrines (etc.) completed. No 3 Sect. also to be employed on Div camp in these sidings.	
	21.		Construction of new camps cont'd. 2 AMIENS huts completed (6 hours). 2 further huts under construction. Well sunk 6 m deep (drum at) J.C.R. COLLOGNE in K.11.b. Further latrines and general camp conveniences erected. No 3 Sect. commenced erection of ADRIAN huts in VILLERS FAUCON 50% of 1 hut being erected. This sect also commenced work on new DIV BATHS at same place. The Cap's Dugout moved to E.236 and former camp there.	
	22.		Work on Spring and effluent trench TIMWORT Rd - commenced (No 2 Sect) work on DIV camp cont'd (No 2 Sect) a further hut complete (8 hours). Well in K.11.b. sunk to 10' on't great water supply obtained confirming expectations based on belief that an excellent water trench could be obtained in chalk throughout length of this valley (COLLOGNE). No 1 Sect proceed to 3 sect in erection of ADRIAN huts 1st hut completed and also for 2nd & 3rd hut level on net levelled.	
	23.		Work on TIMWORT Spring and effluent trench completed. Erection of motor driven shown HEDGE pump.	

WAR DIARY or INTELLIGENCE SUMMARY

Army Form C. 2118.
VOL 23 S.S. 5.

Place	Date	Hour	Summary of Events and Information	Remarks and references to Appendices
VILLERS FAUCON, ST EMILIE, & ROISEL	APRIL 23 (contd)		at SUZANNE WELL ST EMILIE. Work on DIV camp contd. 1 hut completed (9 tables) Erection of ADRIAN huts contd 1 at that ready for erection. Order for 4-5' pipers. Aus DIV telegraph mark ready for use. Work relation on clearing an enemy dugout (followed) at X roads near TEMPLEUX la FOSSE CHURCH. Surfaces to be enriched with 4' deep "change over" road within cross to the way on each. Company transport moved from TINCOURT and passed coy at E.23.c.	
	24		2nd & 3rd ADRIAN huts at VILLER FAUCON completed 50%. Epishing machinery and remover to permit erection of pump platform at ST EMILIE well. Bottom of mine shaft at TEMPLEUX-la-FOSSE reached at 19' and a gallery (timber work) formed to run towards centre of road. 40 yds of camouflage ocean sunk on E. end of ROISEL - ST EMILIE Rd. at new DIV 42 camp.	
	25		2nd & 3rd ADRIAN huts 80% complete. Platform for pump at ST EMILIE well 90% complete. Start made on clearing out other pump well in BRICKFIELD on K.11.C. 90' run of horse trough erected (30' in ST EMILIE and 60' in VILLER FAUCON) 1 position hut erected in DIV camp (10 ft hut) also 48'x12' hut in TINCOURT for Bde H.Q. Extensions to DIV huts VILLER FAUCON completed giving a trailing capacity of 1000 men per day. Gallery of mine at TEMPLEUX la FOSSE cleared 8'. 90 yds (total) of camouflage ocean erected at DIV. H.Q.	
	26.		2nd, 3rd ADRIAN huts completed. Order for 5th, 6th huts taken out and distributed. End of mine gallery	

WAR DIARY
or
INTELLIGENCE SUMMARY
(Erase heading not required.)

Army Form C. 2118.

VOL 23 SN 6

Place	Date	Hour	Summary of Events and Information	Remarks and references to Appendices
VILLERS FAUCON, ST EMILIE, M. ROISEL & TEMPLEUX la FOSSE.	APRIL 26	(cont)	at TEMPLEUX la FOSSE Nissen hut charge of 330 lbs of gun cotton "PERDITE" rammed and detonated by tamping. Two rounds of firing charge had been pushed in; fuse and electrical and both failed. Pump filled at ST EMILIE well. 3' of clr'ns rammed from tubing water level in BRICKFIELD well 80' further — havoc hanging over tubes (60' at ST EMILIE and 20' at VILLERS FAUCON). Also 80' of 1½" outfitting pipe (?) - hose to troughs at VILLERS F. 150 yds (total) of camouflage screen erected at DIV. H.Q.	
	27		4th & 5th ADRIAN huts 75% complete and one for 7 ton lorry out and levelled. Engine pitted to Morr pump at ST EMILIE well. Second element to pump; chain trucking and falling to bottom of well (130') and eventually recovered. 6' of clr'ns rammed from below water level at BRICKFIELDS well and a 25' staging for pump and engine erected. Steam shed at New DIV. R.E. site ST EMILIE commenced.	
	28		4th & 5th ADRIAN huts completed. Chain of pump at ST EMILIE well refixed and replaced. 36rd min unsuccessfully (while insulation had to be taken out horizontally at 11 pm owing to outburst of fire on account of similar through shell fire. BRICKFIELD well cleared of clr'ns to 9' below water level. 1 further hut completed at DIV. camp (11 to date) exclusive of 3 NISSEN huts — 14 in all.	

Army Form C. 2118.

WAR DIARY
or
INTELLIGENCE SUMMARY.
(Erase heading not required.)

VOL 23 Sh 7

Instructions regarding War Diaries and Intelligence Summaries are contained in F. S. Regs., Part II. and the Staff Manual respectively. Title pages will be prepared in manuscript.

Place	Date	Hour	Summary of Events and Information	Remarks and references to Appendices
VILLERS FAUCON ST EMILIE NR ROISEL	APRIL 29		6th Divn had completed 7th hut 50% complete. 50% of pumping plant re-installed at ST EMILIE well (nearest pumping might amount to jobs). Well at BRICKFIELDS cleaned to 12' below water level. Shed for well above at New DIV RE Stores ST EMILIE 9/10 complete.	
	30		7th Divn had completed 8th hut 50% complete. Re-installation of pumping plant at ST EMILIE well completed and 50% of shaping for pumping plant erected at BRICKFIELDS well. 50% of ohs ig for pumping plant erected at BRICKFIELDS well.

The outstanding feature of the month was the continuance of the attrited onslaught of work when the enemy advance on IV Army front commenced, this coy in common with all other RE Field coys which joined BEF came the war of movement. Current the battle of the AISNE, came into its own after the long period of trench warfare during which the field coys had little opportunity of practising their legitimate work, being of necessity, too often employed on tasks which normally should have been undertaken by the infantry. The opportunity thus afforded of carrying their proper function armed have found all RE nearer to a keen appreciation of the care and foresight with which the establishment of a field coy had been drawn up in "peace times" with no regards to personnel and equipment. For practically every job the men and his tools could be found. Despite the weather conditions, which mild all in an April were exceptionally severe for the time of the year, the health of the men remained good and generally they were more comfortably off — certainly in rigorous conditions of work. All round there was general appreciation | |

1577 Wt. W10791/1773 500,000 1/15 D. D. & L. A.D.S.S./Forms/C. 2118.

WAR DIARY
INTELLIGENCE SUMMARY.
(Erase heading not required.)

Army Form C. 2118.

VOL 23 S & 2.

Place	Date	Hour	Summary of Events and Information	Remarks and references to Appendices

After more trenches were left behind and consequently "clean" country advanced into. The nature of mind with which we could be said to have been in any rapid advance the [proximity?] the absolute thoroughness of the enemies "outfires" in their work of harrying our advance was on the nature of a surprise to some of us. Even admitting that months of "preparatory" work must have been available the [?] careful examination for their thoroughness and energy. Practically nothing that could be done was left undone, and no ingenuity was wasted by the continued explosions of "[?] mines" at irregular intervals — in some cases more than a month after we had crossed on area. These were so carefully concealed — normally in culverts of fillube [?] leading to be used by troops — that in several cases they exploded amount by efforts after information as to their appropriate location had been obtained from prisoners. In every instance they were possibly operated by the electro-chemical detonating device mentioned in DIARY for March. The prevalence of these "traps" led to a general movement of troops into bivouacs we [?] around in 18 and continued good weather to date was more the change in [?] as all normal. The nature of work done by R.E. units as shown in duty entries

The most important traits were the [?] of communications and water supply for men & horses from opening wells & follows by [?] of successions for troops. In this latter connection the specialties of the "ADRIAN"

WAR DIARY
or
INTELLIGENCE SUMMARY.
(Erase heading not required.)

Army Form C. 2118.

VOL 23 Sh 9.

Place	Date	Hour	Summary of Events and Information	Remarks and references to Appendices

discovered afterward. These abandoned hutts (of which a number were left made by the French when we took over from them south of the Somme early this year) all needing interior clean and re-wired where required. I had hutts into five 3 ton lorries and only required about 18 men 2 days to re-erect. Each hut gives ample accommodation for 130 men. 4 of a sect. (No 4) were detailed also (in out to HAMEL (nr CERISY) and later moved to CERISY. At both of these places they experimented in taking down of these huts by working further parties by Corps artillery. Experience proved that much time was saved in re-erection of a good system of marking the elements of each hut was followed when taking them down.

As regards WATER SUPPLY the efficiency and simplicity of the tell-and-chain water lifting pumps was effectually demonstrated. Both types are substantially the same and are capable of raising water practically any depth. They depend for their action on an endless chain (carried by pulleys) on 8" canvas balls running over a pulley at well head, the balls kept running in contact with the of water which is carried up adhering to them in bell and thrown off at pulley a well head by centrifugal force when it is collected by a tank which enclosed pulley. These pumps were mainly driven by petrol motors of 5 h.p. 1½" gate I/pump being the average quantity of fuel required to raise 5000 galls in 6 hours.

A.F.MacLennan Lt
Asst A.D.S.S 477 Fd Co RE

WAR DIARY
or
INTELLIGENCE SUMMARY.
(Erase heading not required.)

Army Form C. 2118.

Instructions regarding War Diaries and Intelligence Summaries are contained in F. S. Regs., Part II. and the Staff Manual respectively. Title pages will be prepared in manuscript.

vol 23 Sheet 10

Summary of Events and Information

Extract from WEEKLY STATES.

Place	Date	Hour	STRENGTH		REINFORCEMENTS		TRANSFERS		KILLED		C.C.S.		Remarks and references to Appendices
			OFF	OR	OFF	OR	FROM	TO			FROM	TO	
	1917												
	Apl. 7		9	219	–	1	–	1*	–	1	1	1	*Returned from H⁹ on Bkings G
	" 14		8	216	–	–	–	–	–	1	2	–	
	" 21		8	215	–	–	–	–	–	1	1	1	Drains & Soundation Smoke Drfit
	" 28		7	217	–	4	1 OR	–]*	–	1	1	–	

Actual Strength
OFF 4 OR 190

			Detached	
			OFF	OR
45ᵗʰ H.Q. R.E.			1	5
" Train			–	2
Leave			2	5
R.E. Stores			–	2
III Corps Nutting			–	13
			3	27

J McIlym
Acting RE
477 Fld Co R.E.

CONFIDENTIAL.

War Diary

— of —

477th (S.M.) Field Co. R.E.

From 1st May 1917 to 31st May 1917.

(Volume 24.)
5 sheets.

WAR DIARY
or
INTELLIGENCE SUMMARY.
(Erase heading not required.)

VOL 24. SHEET 1.

Army Form C. 2118.

Place	Date	Hour	Summary of Events and Information	Remarks and references to Appendices
VILLERS-FAUCON	MAY 1		Breakdown of "Claire Helice" pump at S'te EMILIE repaired. 8 It'd ADRIAN huts complete. Screen at Div. Hq camouflaged. Fire at S'te EMILIE suerarie finally extinguished.	
	2		Engine at well at water point VILLERS FAUCON failed owing to too constant use. Wholly dismantled & put in running order by morning. 200 gallon tank erected at S'te EMILIE. Standby for ambulation lorry made.	
	3		Cage for prisoners at RSC 63 completed. Repairing of huts, general works in stores.	
	4		Horse trough repaired 30ft new trough erected at S'te EMILIE. Repairs to huts and water lifting gear. Hut erected for G.O.C. 42nd Div R.A. at Div. Hq.	
	5		100 ft horse trough erected at VILLERS-FAUCON. 2 Pumps (hand) installed at reservoir S'te EMILIE. Armed hut in ADRIAN HUT at VILLERS-FAUCON destroyed 6 trays. 1 N.C.O. killed as result of shelling. 190 ft horse trough erected at MARQUAIX. Extension to bath VILLERS-FAUCON 30% complete.	
	6		Work on "BROWN LINE" begun. New engine arrived for water lifter. 300 ft horse trough erected at Div. Hq. 80 ft additional trough erected at MARQUAIX also standing for water cart made. Extension blocks 60% complete.	

Army Form C. 2118.

WAR DIARY
or
INTELLIGENCE SUMMARY.
(Erase heading not required.)

VOL. 24. SHEET 2.

Place	Date	Hour	Summary of Events and Information	Remarks and references to Appendices
	7		Storage tank (1790 gall.) erected at Nre EMILIE for sterilized water. Extension to baths 80% complete. Names of various villages painted on walls. New engine erected on temporary bed. 100 ft additional troughing erected at MARQUAIX. 30 ft troughing erected at TINCOURT. Various carpentry work in stores.	
	8		Extension to div. baths completed. Various carpentry work in stores. 70 metres troughs made & painted.	
	9		Reinforced concrete bed laid for engine at VILLERS FAUCON water point. Damaged ADRIAN HUT 50% repaired. 2 NISSEN HUTS erected at LONGAVESNES. Capacity of well (supposed by some to be a reservoir) tested, water level not lowered by 6 hours pumping continuously for 6 hours. ADRIAN HUT 75% complete. 3 sets goal posts for WD Bn made. 2 additional NISSEN HUTS erected at LONGAVESNES.	
	10			
	12		Major Briggs resumed command. Company moved to PERONNE. Officer left with W.O & Driv. in charge of BROWN LINE.	
PERONNE	15		Company moved to COMBLES.	
COMBLES	16		Company moved to and took over headquarters at LEBUCQUIERE.	
LEBUCQUIERE	17		Reconnoitred work etc.	

Army Form C. 2118.

WAR DIARY
or
INTELLIGENCE SUMMARY.
(Erase heading not required.)

VOL 24. SHEET 3.

Place	Date	Hour	Summary of Events and Information	Remarks and references to Appendices
	18		Right Brigade reserve line reconnoitered. Dumps of wiring material formed. Drive across canal at J36b82 15% complete. Work on wells in HERMIES and DOIGNES. Work on baths at VELU.	
	19.		DEFENCES. Part 18 wired tactically. Canal dam 30% completed. Work on wells continued. Baths, VELU continued; HAPLINCOURT material collected & hauled to site.	
	20.		DEFENCES. 470ˣ tactical wire erected. Post R.R.2 extended 100ˣ. Work on dams & wells handed over to 474 Field Co RE.	
	21.		DEFENCES. 410ˣ wire erected. O.P for 240 Brigade R.F.A. K25 a 2.5 sited & begun. Reconnaissance of front line posts R.1 - 9 made. Wire found to be rather poor & in own avisiant[?].	
	22		~~~~~~ R.F.A. O.P. 20% completed. Clearing of roads thro' HERMIES and DOIGNES begun. Tracks from EE Hty J18b·19 to support posts RD1 & RD2. Reconnaissance of front line posts R.9 - 15 made. Wire torn. 210ˣ wire erected on R.R. line. Work stopped after 2 hours owing to gas (own)	
	23.		alarm. Site for 2ⁿᵈ R.F.A. O.P. K25 a 32 selected & work begun. Clearing of roads cont'd. Work restarted on canal dam.	

1577 Wt. W10791/1773 500,000 1/15 D. D. & L.   A.D.S.S./Forms/C. 2118.

WAR DIARY or INTELLIGENCE SUMMARY

Army Form C. 2118.

Vol. 24 Sheet 4.

Place	Date	Hour	Summary of Events and Information	Remarks and references to Appendices
LEBUCQUIERE	1917 May 24		DEFENCES. Front line posts. 50 yds of new front line dug, old trenches improved. Reserve line 2000 yds of "Tactical" line erected up to date. Trenches retained & improved.	France 57c N.E. Sh. 3.A. 1/20,000
	" 25		O.P's. Work continued. ROADS. Cleared through DOIGNIES & HERMIES.	
	" 25	6	Work continued as above.	
	" 31		DEFENCES. Front line posts. 92 yds of new front line dug & old trenches further improved. Reserve line. "Tactical" line 3330 yds erected up to date, 485 yds of defensive wire strengthened to depth of 24'. Trenches further retained & improved. O.P's. completed for 2 Div Fd. R.F.A. at K25a.6.2.; J30.6.58.; K7c.76.; and K25a.63. Dugouts in connection with OP's started. Work continued on HERMIES ROADS. Canal dam J.36.6.8.2. completed.	

Army Form C. 2118

WAR DIARY
or
INTELLIGENCE SUMMARY
(Erase heading not required.)

Vol 24 sheet 5.

Summary of Events and Information

EXTRACTS FROM WEEKLY STATES

DATE 1917	STRENGTH		REINFORTS		TRANSFERS		KILLED		CAS	
	Off.	O.R.	Off.	O.R.	From	To			From	To
May 5	8	226	1	9						
" 12	8	224				1 (×)		(0)		
" 19	8	223								
" 26	8	221				1 (3)				

(×) II Cpl E.J. PRICE appointed
    SGH Sgt. A/F/M
(2) L/Cpl G.T.S. Cox
(3) Spr. CULVER HYDE G.
    Inv'l'd for Commission

ACTUAL STRENGTH
Off.	O.R.
6	206

DETACHED
	Off.	O.R.
48th Div. HQ R.E.		3
train		2
leave		3
Hospital	1	6
477 Det C. R.E.	1	1
TOTAL	2	15

May 26

D Whyte
Major
O.C. 477 Fd Coy R.E.

CONFIDENTIAL.

WAR DIARY

of

477th (S.M.) Field Company.

Royal Engineers.

From 1st June 1917 To 30th June 1917.

(Volume 25)
(Sheets 6)

Army Form C. 2118

WAR DIARY
or
INTELLIGENCE SUMMARY
(Erase heading not required.)

VOL. 25 sheet 1

Place	Date	Hour	Summary of Events and Information	Remarks and references to Appendices
LEBUCQUIERE	JUNE 1.		Wiring on Reserve line & digging of communication trenches continued. Small parties employed on roads in BEAUMETZ von BEAUMETZ - DOIGNIES. Owing to scarcity of men available, only the worst holes were filled in.	TRENCH MAP. HERMIES 57c NE 3 Edition IA 1:10,000.
	3.		Defensive wire on Reserve line continued. Support communication trenches dug to depth of 1'6" nine. It was not proposed to dig these trenches any deeper until such time as the whole defensive scheme of the Reserve line had been mapped out on the ground.	
			Major Bragg received D.S.O. in Birthday Honours list.	
	4.		Work on Reserve line continued, principally tactical & defensive wiring. Various OPs & dugouts connected with them in hand at K.25.a.50.40 called RFA OP North, K.25 a.55.20 - Bde. OP South - K.25 a.50.30 - Road OP. The existing dugout at Bde OP South was extended to act as a dugout also for RFA OP South at K.25.a.55.23	
	7.		Dumps for Brigade were chiefly mess forms at J.30.b.59 & J.16.b.66 materials stores herein	

WAR DIARY
or
INTELLIGENCE SUMMARY
(Erase heading not required.)

Army Form C. 2118

Vol 25 sheet 2.

Place	Date	Hour	Summary of Events and Information	Remarks and references to Appendices
LEBUCQUIERE	JUNE 7th Cont		A sketch map showing positions of points OPs in K 25a 10 attached. An additional OP in house in HERMIES village at J 30 b 58 was also constructed, a small dugout with 2 entrances, — one being a vertical shaft, made under the house. Some trenches near Bn OP South also at cross roads J 20 c 83 near Brigade HQ.	TRENCH MAP HERMIES 57c NE 3 Edition 1A 1:10,000.
	8.		During the night 7/8 a raid was made by 1st Bucks Batt" from Post 3 – K 26 a 82 – on enemy post S of SLAG HEAP. II/Lt A.G. MACLENNAN, II Corps Mines Sapper Take were detailed to have at trenches & enemy wire then the post had been occupied. A Company of S.W.Royal Sussex men detailed to B dig the trenches necessary. The operation was a complete success, the entire enemy post being either killed or captured. Their position consolidated wire; the German NCO commanding the post was captured by L/Cpl MACLENNAN to whose initiative in laying out & forming up tapes for the attacking party and for work on his organisation of digging wiring parties the success of the operation was very largely due.	

WAR DIARY or INTELLIGENCE SUMMARY

Army Form C. 2118

Vol 25 sheet 3.

Place	Date	Hour	Summary of Events and Information	Remarks and references to Appendices
LEBUCQUIERE	JUNE 14		Defensive tactical wiring on Reserve line continued. RFA North OP continued 149 frames strong now inplace. Dugout in Bn OP South completed. A new piece of dugouts for 145 Inf Brigade was started in small quarry at J 24 a 72 for Command post. 300″ revetting at J 30 c 83 completed. Revetting round Bn OP South restricted mainly where damaged by shell fire. Work on BEAUMETZ - HERMIES road continued with small parties on footways across canal Du NORD at J 36 b 83 complete. Bridging material - collected from ruined village in the vicinity - made up into trestles to take 8 ton loads. These were [in use] in case of an advance across canal Du NORD. After spending 6 days on this work, it was found that superior authority had already collected material of bridges for this particular purpose.	TRENCH MAP HERMIES 57c NE 3 1:10,000
	19.		An additional company of 5th Royal Sussex were attached toward to Reserve line the following posts were dug to full depth. 1A. 2. 3. 4. 6. 7. 10. 14.	
	23		Posts on Reserve line dug to depth in addition to above are 5, 9, 47. Field ovens were erected for the use of garrisons in posts 7, 9, 10, 11, 13.	

1875 Wt. W593/826 1,000,000 4/15 J.B.C. & A. A.D.S.S./Forms/C. 2118.

Army Form C. 2118

WAR DIARY
or
INTELLIGENCE SUMMARY
(Erase heading not required.)

VOL 25 sheet 4.

Place	Date	Hour	Summary of Events and Information	Remarks and references to Appendices
LEBUCQUIERE	June 25.		Posts 8.11.12.13.15.16.18 19 Dug to full depth. 650' communication trench Dug to depth of 1' in connection with support reserve lines of these posts. Dugouts were started by Sprees in Posts 1A & 2 - dugouts for RFA North OP - 313 cases - 145 Brigade Command Post - 254 cases - 31 6'x6' frames to use in addition to above work 240 screw pins sorted in quarry at Confurst. T.24 a.7.9., a chair, helice mill in Doignies at T.16.a 55 was dismantled together with madrass - a good mill in Demicourt at T.18.b 40 cleaned out trenches on VELU - BEAUMETZ - BEAUMETZ - BEAUMETZ - HERMIES road to make rover posts. Work on VELU - BEAUMETZ - BEAUMETZ - HERMIES road continued. Lt. MACLENNAN received Military Cross for his work on the evening 7/8th.	TRENCH MAP HERMIES 57c NE 3 1:10,000
	31.		Dugouts for RFA North OP 145 Brigade OP. also 145 Brigade Command Post complete. Total number of cases & frames used - RFA OP. 381 - 6'x3'. 37 - 4'x3'. 145 Command Post 341 - 6'x3'. 32 - 6'x4'. 33 - 6'x6'.	

1875 Wt. W593/826 1,000,000 4/15 J.B.C. & A. A.D.S.S./Forms/C. 2118.

Army Form C. 2118.

Vol 25 Shet 5

WAR DIARY
or
INTELLIGENCE SUMMARY.
(Erase heading not required.)

Place	Date	Hour	Summary of Events and Information	Remarks and references to Appendices

Extracts from Weekly States.

Date	Strength Off	Strength OR	Reinforcements Off	Reinforcements OR	Transfers From Off	Transfers From OR	Transfers To Off	Transfers To OR	Killed Off	Killed OR	C.C.S. From	C.C.S. To	Remarks
2/6/17	1	220	-	-	-	-	-	1	-	-	-	-	No 2 Base Rouen
9/6/17	1	221	-	1	-	-	-	-	-	-	1	1	
16/6/17	1	221	-	-	-	-	-	-	-	-	1	1	
23/6/17	1	221	-	2	-	-	-	-	-	-	-	2	
29/6/17	1	223	-	2	-	-	-	-	-	-	-	-	

Actual Strength on June 29.

Off	OR
1	207

Detailed Off OR
- HQ Bn R.E. — 3
- " " Train — 1
- Leave — 4
- Army Rest Camp — 1
- Hospital — 5
- 149 Ft C.R.E — 2/16

Army Form C. 2118.

Vol. 25 Sheet 6

WAR DIARY
or
INTELLIGENCE SUMMARY.
(Erase heading not required.)

Instructions regarding War Diaries and Intelligence Summaries are contained in F.S. Regs., Part II. and the Staff Manual respectively. Title pages will be prepared in manuscript.

Place	Date	Hour	Summary of Events and Information	Remarks and references to Appendices

The following figures give casualties, reinforcements, transfers etc. in both men & horses from the original company to at landing 6/6/15 up 6/6/17.

	(1) STRENGTH		(2) REINFORCEMENTS		(3) TOTAL		(4) TRANSFERS, C.C.S. etc. or other units				(5) KILLED, DIED OF WOUNDS DIED ORIG. Co. REINFORCEMENTS				(6) TOTAL (3)-(4)-(5)		(7) CASUALTIES REJOINING UNIT ORIG. Co. REINFORCEMENTS			
	OFF.	O.R.	OFF.	O.R.	OFF.	O.R.	OFF.	O.R.	OFF.	O.R.	OFF.	O.R.	OFF.	O.R.	OFF.	O.R.	OFF.	O.R.	OFF.	O.R.
STRENGTH AT 6.6.15	6	211																		
" 6.6.16	7	224	4	68	10	219	1	50	2	15		6			7	208	-	14	-	2
" 6.6.17	7	220	4	64	11	288	2	51	2	31		4		5	7	199	-	13	-	3
STRENGTH OF ORIGINAL Co AT 6.6.16	5	169																		
" AT 6.6.17	3	132																		

HORSES

STRENGTH AT 6.6.16.	79
CASUALTIES	21
REINFORCEMENTS	21
STRENGTH ORIGINAL Co.	58

AT 6.6.17
19
26
22
43

D.Whipp
Major
O.C. 477 Fd. Co. R.E.

7/17

1577 Wt W10791/1773 500,000 1/15 D. D. & L. A.D.S.S./Forms/C. 2118.

Vol 26

War Diary
477 (S.M) Field Coy R.E.

Vol 26 - (3 sheets)
From 1/7/17 to 31/7/17

Army Form C. 2118.

Vol 26 sheet 1

WAR DIARY
or
INTELLIGENCE SUMMARY.
(Erase heading not required.)

Instructions regarding War Diaries and Intelligence Summaries are contained in F. S. Regs., Part II. and the Staff Manual respectively. Title pages will be prepared in manuscript.

Place	Date	Hour	Summary of Events and Information	Remarks and references to Appendices
	1917			
LEBUCQUIERE	July 1	1 pm	Handed over all work to 57th Field Co. R.E.	
			Moved to BIHUCOURT arriving 4 pm, no billets arranged when moving under Inf. Bde. orders	
BIHUCOURT	2/4		Resting. Inspected by G.O.C. 48th Div. 7pm July 4	
	5	2-30 pm	Moved to ACHIET le GRAND	
		4-0 am	Entrained at ACHIET le GRAND for move to + VIII Corps area.	
	6	11-30 am	Arrival at HOPOUTRE (POPERINGHE)	
		2-0	Moved to bivouacs in wood A.24.d.4.2. For a hundred 5 days rest	Belgium 28NW
	7		1st day's rest. Shelled with long range H.V. guns 2 men wounded 2 horses killed.	
		12 md	Moved to camp 300 yards away, also shells during night no casualties.	
	8	2 pm	2nd day's rest. Moved to camp on POPERINGHE-WATOU road, ¼ mile from HOPOUTRE	
	9/10		Rest, but we detained on July 6th time taken to move the distance 52½ hrs.	
	11	5 pm	Nos 1 & 4 sections to forward billets, No 1 & 8 Hts. 6.34 near BURGOMASTER farm to work in forward tunnel, RAMC collecting post under CRE 39th Div.	
	12	2 pm	H.Q's not seen & all transport to camp A.10.87 POP. HOESTEN road	

1577 Wt.W10791/1773 500,000 1/15 D. D. & L. A.D.S.S./Forms/C. 2118.

WAR DIARY
or
INTELLIGENCE SUMMARY.
(Erase heading not required.)

Army Form C. 2118.

Vol 26 sheet 2

Place	Date	Hour	Summary of Events and Information	Remarks and references to Appendices
POPERINGHE	1917 July 25		3 sections on forward work & 1 sec. in H.Q. camp. Location relieved every 4 days. Very few proper made owing to intense enemy gas shelling. Forward track hauled out from CANAL BANK bridge 2H to front line track. Some work done in filling shell holes, & generally improving track. One large French steel shelter erected & excavation made for a second. Heavy casualties due to shell fire & particularly gas shells. Total KILLED 1 WOUNDED 18 WOUNDED, GAS. 49. Several of the wounded gas men died later.	
	"26/29		The whole company at H.Q. camp, resting, training, Making panniers etc. for pack transport, training pack animals, Hauling material to East side of CANAL for work on forward track on Z day.	
	" 24		21 Reinforcements received	
	" 28		43 ib. ib.	
	" 30 4 p.m		H.Q's & 4 sections moved to forward bivouacs H44C (Belgium 27 N W)	
	" 31 3-50 a.m.		At zero hour leaders, D¹ MACLENNAN & McD. from R.ack. section reconn. out forward track from HAMMOND'S CORNER, South of HILLTOP FARM to ADMIRAL'S ROAD	

WAR DIARY
or
INTELLIGENCE SUMMARY.
(Erase heading not required.)

Army Form C. 2118.

Vol 26 sheet 3.

Place	Date	Hour	Summary of Events and Information	Remarks and references to Appendices
Camp H.W.C.	1917 July 31		Slight change in HILLTOP PIKETT delayed reconnaissance slightly, however arr'd back at 5-45 a.m. Cooling up sections, all were at work at 8-15 a.m & the track was completed & passable for all kind transport at 2 p.m. Work ceased at 3-15 p.m.	

EXTRACTS from WEEKLY STATES

Date	Strength Off.	Strength O.R.	Reinforcements Off.	Reinforcements O.R.	Transfers Off.	Transfers O.R.	Killed Off.	Killed O.R.	Cas Off.	Cas O.R.	
July 7	8	223	–	–	–	–	–	–	–	7	
" 14	7	220	–	–	–	–	–	–	1	1	*Capt Cecil Pond E. Commnd 477 Fd Co.
" 21	7	212	–	4	–	–	–	–	1	3	
" 28	6	200	–	21	–	–	–	–	1	11	
										34*	*4 Light Duty Acc. wounded

Major
O.C. 477 Fd. Co. R.E.

CONFIDENTIAL

WAR DIARY

of

477th E.M. Field Company R.E.

From 1st August 1917 to 31st August 1917.

(Volume 27)
Sheets 6

Vol 27

145 Inf. Bde. O.P.

23' HEAD COVER

30'

NORTH O.P.
240 Bde. R.F.A.

10'

15'

22'

20' HEAD COVER

63'

"ROAD" O.P.
2 OBSERVERS

120'

20' HEAD COVER

N ← MAGNETIC

SAND PIT.

HERMIES – HAVRINCOURT ROAD.

SCALE 15' = 1"

Army Form C. 2118.

Vol 27 Sheet 1.

WAR DIARY
or
INTELLIGENCE SUMMARY.
(Erase heading not required.)

Place	Date	Hour	Summary of Events and Information	Remarks and references to Appendices
Canal Bank H.Q.C.	1917 Aug 1		Work continued on BATH ROAD, fair weather but to ADMIRAL'S ROAD. Weather not looking deteriorating hourly & will soon become impassable unless weather improves or traffic diminishes. 10ft of OR's employed clear of traffic. Unable to continue work upon it unless weather.	ST. JULIEN 28 N.W. 2.
	" 2		BATH road improves greatly. Formation made for WESTBOUND track 750 yds, from IRISH FARM to BUFF'S ROAD C21.d.14.	
	" 3		Track bonds laid on formation made yesterday. 2 sections resting.	
	" 4		400 yds of Westbound track made + laid. Complete. 2 " "	
	" 5		400 yds of Westbound track made + laid. Complete 2 " "	
	" 5 3pm		hours 6. 234 fd. Co. billets EAST CANAL BANK C.25.d.38.	
	" 6		Worked on BATH road forward of ADMIRAL'S ROAD. 2 " "	
			2 OR's wounded.	
Canal Bank N. of YPRES	" 7		Work continued on BATH H. road. 2 OR's wounded.	

WAR DIARY
or
INTELLIGENCE SUMMARY.
(Erase heading not required.)

Army Form C. 2118.

Vol 27. Sheet 2.

Place	Date	Hour	Summary of Events and Information	Remarks and references to Appendices
CANAL BANK N. of YPRES	1917 Aug 7		Work started on tramway from ADMIRAL'S ROAD C.13.d.60. to south corner of KITCHENER'S ROAD, a length of 1600 yards.	
	" 8		Work continued on BATHS ROAD & tramway. 650 yds of formation completed including bridges & cross drains. 1 O.R. wounded. Work continued as above. 1 O.R. wounded.	
	" 9		[sketch of trench/road cross-section with dimensions 2'3", 2'3", 8", 1']	
	" 10		800 yds of formation completed, 340 yds of track laid. 240 yds of trackboards laid below rails.	
	" 11		Work carried on BATHS ROAD. Owing to the continued wet weather, also on tramway owing to all available men being required to prepare hard cut infantry tracks, 2 more 475 H.C. attached for this purpose.	
			① Track from BATH BRG CAMP to bridge 3a & forward N. of HAMMONDS CORNER & HILL TOP to ADMIRAL'S ROAD.	
			② Track from DAMBRE CAMP to bridge 2a.	

Army Form C. 2118.

Vol 27 Sheet 3.

WAR DIARY
or
INTELLIGENCE SUMMARY.
(Erase heading not required.)

Instructions regarding War Diaries and Intelligence Summaries are contained in F.S. Regs., Part II. and the Staff Manual respectively. Title pages will be prepared in manuscript.

Place	Date	Hour	Summary of Events and Information	Remarks and references to Appendices
CANAL BANK N. of YPRES	1917 Aug 12		"Bo. do". trench practically completed	
	13		2. P. over copse built @ HILLTOP C.21.d.58 (b) Bridge 2.a. Trench board track REIGERSBERG to bridge 3 & towards HAMMOND'S CORNER 180 yds made & laid (8 section R.E.) 1 O.R. wounded	
	14		Above track continued N. of HAMMOND'S CORNER, N. of HILLTOP to ADMIRAL'S ROAD C.21.6.69. 290 & 280 formation made, 2300 yds track boards laid (at every R.E. & no S.g.) 1 O.R. killed 1 wounded	
	15		Above track completed. 600 yds track boards laid & all damage repaired. 1 O.R. killed 2 O.R. wounded	
	16		145 Inf. Bde attacked at 4.45 a.m. Saps attached to 475 Tnl.Coy. for consolidation. 3 sectors continued work on tramway. 3 O.R. wounded	
	17/19		3 sections at work on tramway, 100 yds of track laid & tramlaid obtained, 1360 yds & formation made.	
	19		1 section completed MoR du HIBOU after attack by 5/6 Norf.	
	20		Concrete dugout in Q.C.1 (CAL.1 RAM & CAL.1 RAM support trench) cleaned, drained & made fit for occupation.	

WAR DIARY / INTELLIGENCE SUMMARY

Army Form C. 2118.

Vol 27 Sheet 4.

Place	Date	Hour	Summary of Events and Information	Remarks
CANAL BANK N. of YPRES	1917 Aug 21	9.0 a.m.	Work continued on accommodation in O.G.1. Excavations started for large French shelters on our side. Enemy dug into concrete dugout. [sketch of dugout profile labeled "concrete dugout / front slab"]	
	22/23/24	7.30 p.m.	Road bridge ST JULIEN over STEENBEEK repaired & made passable for tanks. Work completed 12 mid.; last tank passed over at 4-40 a.m. Aug 22. [sketch showing enemy side/our side with concrete dugout]	
	23		Work continued on accommodation in O.G.1. Area between STEENBEEK & ST JULIEN - LANGEMARCK road searched for accommodation. O.G. dugouts, firepits &c. Work carried out during night. The section parties by day in the accommodation holes good & continuing until next night. Assembly trenches covered with camouflage for proposed day attack by 144 Inf. Bde. Road 600 yds of track covered with camouflage, hire netting & canvas strips, during the nights 24/25, 25/26 & 26/27. Infantry in position 2 a.m. Aug 27. The camouflage was a complete success, no	
	25		of the troops being detected by the enemy during this 12 hours stay in daylight under the camouflage, tho' enemy aeroplanes reconnoitred the ground daily, flying very low, 200/300 feet.	

Army Form C. 2118.

WAR DIARY
or
INTELLIGENCE SUMMARY.
(Erase heading not required.)

Vol 27 Sheet 5

Place	Date	Hour	Summary of Events and Information	Remarks and references to Appendices
CANAL BANK N. of YPRES.	1917 Aug 26th		Work continued on accommodation in O.G.1 & on Blockhouse 150 yds E. of MIBOU "80"	
	27	1.55 am	Attack by 144 Inf. Bde. met weather the previous night & during the day of attack seriously interfered with the operations, the going over the sodden shelled ground being almost impossible.	
			1 Section standing by in O.G.1. for consolidation of VANCOUVER.	
		5.30	Lt BRIGGS party went forward to reconnoitre to A.2.B5.R.2A.	
		6.45	Section moved forward	
		8.30	Situation found to be very obscure, Germans undoubtedly in possession of SPRINGFIELD + probably VANCOUVER	
		9.30	Section returned to billets	
	"28		Work continued on accommodation in O.G.1. & forward tramway repaired.	
	29		Relieved by 503 Fd. Co. Broken billets fall work was handed over.	
CAMP G.6.a.57.		am 10.0	Company moved to Camp G.6.a.57. 4000 yds E. of POPERINGHE.	Belgium 28mv.
G.6.a.57.	31		Military hiked admitted to ICpl F.J. JONES by XVIII Corps Commander for work stated, erection of huts at SIEGE CAMP B.20.d.57.	

WAR DIARY
or
INTELLIGENCE SUMMARY.
(Erase heading not required.)

Army Form C. 2118.

Vol 27 Sheet 6.

Place	Date	Hour	Summary of Events and Information	Remarks and references to Appendices
	Aug		The operations during this month were distinguished by alternate periods of wet & fine weather, the latter hardly ever being sufficiently long to repair the damage done by the wet, being more almost impossible, the difficulty of maintaining communications almost insuperable, the Dry trench bomb Hordes End were invaluable.	
			Extract from Weekly State	
			Strength Reinforcements Transfers KILLED Cas.
			Offr. O.R. Offr. O.R. From To From To Offr. O.R.	
	Aug 4		5 235 1 7	× Lt Pennington invalided
	11		6 226 43 1 9	2/Lieut Roby 2nd E.L.G.
	18		6 218 1 2 6	
	25		6 208 4 6	

Whyte
Major
O.C. 477 2nd Co. R.E.

SECRET

War Diary

— of —

477th South Midland Field Coy.
Royal Engineers.

From 1st Sep 1917 to 30th Sep. 1917.

(Volume No 28)
(Sheets. 21)

Vol 28

Army Form C. 2118.

Vol 28 Sheet 1

WAR DIARY
or
INTELLIGENCE SUMMARY.
(Erase heading not required.)

Instructions regarding War Diaries and Intelligence Summaries are contained in F.S. Regs., Part II. and the Staff Manual respectively. Title pages will be prepared in manuscript.

Place	Date	Hour	Summary of Events and Information	Remarks and references to Appendices
Camp P 61.a.57	1917 Sept 1	6	Work continued on erection of NISSEN HUTS at SIEGE CAMP B20 d.57. In 10 days 31 huts were completed, 25444 man hours being worked, the average for the period being 82 man hours per hut, this includes all delays due to lack of material etc. The present days work has 5 huts in 300 man hours = 60 man hours per hut.	Belgium 28 N.W.
	" 9		Major E. BRIGGS away on leave in PARIS	
	Sept 7/11		Training. No.1 section	
	" 10/14		Hq's & No.104 section moved to PROVEN to with under CRE 5th Army troops	HAZE BROUCK 5a 3.a 88.
	" 15 9am		No.s 2 + 3 section moved to ST JANSTER MEZEN attached No.4 Inf. Bde.	
	" 17 5pm		No.s 2 & 3 sections moved by rail to LA RECOUSSE for RE Annexe in that area	
	- 16		No.s 104 section working on hutting at CCS's M. B.p.p. 47 and at CRE depot PROVEN workshops.	
	- 22		Lt L. BRIGGS rejoined the Company from RE Base Depot ROUEN	
	- 23		Lt L. BRIGGS proceeded on leave to England	
	- 28 10am		Hq's & No.104 section moved to PETEZ HOEK Camp A 21.a.87	A 21 a 87

1577 Wt.W10791/1773 500,000 1/15 D.D. & L. A.D.S.S./Forms/C. 2118.

Army Form C. 2118.

WAR DIARY
or
INTELLIGENCE SUMMARY.
(Erase heading not required.)

Vol 28 Sheet 2

Place	Date	Hour	Summary of Events and Information	Remarks and references to Appendices
	1917			
PESET. HOEK	Sep 30	10 am	H.Q's and 1+4 sections moved to billets in EAST CANAL BANK Forward area. reconnoitred preparatory to starting work.	

	STRENGTH		REINFORCEMENTS		TRANSFERS		STATES KILLED		C.C.S	
date	OFF.	O.R.	OFF.	O.R.	FROM	TO			FROM	TO	
Aug 31	5	205	-	-	-	-	-	-	2	5	
Sep 7	6	201	1	1	-	1	-	-	1	4	
" 14	6	202	1	4	2	1*	-	-	1	2	*Cpl Cave to England
" 28	6	199	-	1	-	-	-	-	1	4	
" 28	6	201	-	4	-	1*	-	-	-	1	*Cpl Stone to England

2/10/17

[signature]
Major
OC 477 Fd Co. RE

CONFIDENTIAL.

WAR DIARY

— of —

477th (S.M.) Field Co. R.E.

(Volume 29)
(Sheets 3)

Army Form C. 2118

Vol. 29 Sheet 1

WAR DIARY
or
INTELLIGENCE SUMMARY
(Erase heading not required.)

Instructions regarding War Diaries and Intelligence Summaries are contained in F. S. Regs., Part II. and the Staff Manual respectively. Title Pages will be prepared in manuscript.

Place	Date	Hour	Summary of Events and Information	Remarks and references to Appendices
EAST CANAL BANK	1917 Oct 1	9	Road from TRIANGLE to HUBNER F.m. reconnoitred. Work of clearing above & filling in shell holes, laying 9 in & R.D. ↑s & sleepers also 2 platoons worked at night on this.	
		5-9	24th Fwd Co R.E. worked under the direction of this Cy.- on R. day - laying clothing trail, clothing laid 426 yds. 350 yds road cleared, shell holes filled & framework made from HUBNER	
	Oct 2-3		Picket crows here erected at 18 points.	
	Oct 1	4	ST JULIEN - WINNIPEG Road made good, shell holes filled, tres places required. 1st platoon of 5th sussex.	
		1-9	1st ST JULIEN - TRIANGLE road repairs maintained by few men. 1st & 3rd sussex.	
		2-6	Tramway E side of TRIANGLE - WINNIPEG Road laid for R.F.A. (4 batteries) 800 yds. Work much impeded by shell fire, a number of direct hits being obtained.	
	Oct 6		10 holes trans erected.	
		2	220 yds trench brass track laid on prolongation from C 6 c 70 to C 6 d 05 10	
			R.E. stores were dumped at JANET FARM dump - none sandbags trans pickets short thickness	
		9	Ford READING at TRIANGLE restored. Men being possible to reach JANET F.m. Stores were dumped alongside "ACE OF HEARTS" tank about C 12 d 03	
		10	Police trans erected at 2 points.	
		10	Rest work & billets handed now to 90th Fld Co R.E.	
	Oct 2	6	O.C. machine-gun returned from leave.	
		10	Lt Briggs returned from leave.	
		10	4 platoons 114 tps moved from CANAL BILLETS to BROWN CAMP. A 23 d 08 sheet 28 NW	Sheet 28 NW
			remainder moved from DAMBRE CAMP to BROWN CAMP.	

WAR DIARY
or
INTELLIGENCE SUMMARY

Army Form C. 2118

Vol 29. Sheet 2

Place	Date	Hour	Summary of Events and Information	Remarks and references to Appendices
BROWN CAMP	1917 Oct 15		Company entrained at PESELHOEK - All horses, vehicles (New Britains) by 8. am.	
	17		Company detained at MARGEVIL - arriving at 3.45 pm. Company marched to RCR line billets Mine.	
	19-31		Company moved to Camp at A1C.6.9 (Sheet 11 NORDEM 5.1.B N W) No. 3 Section erected 2 Nissen huts near "CURIOS" No. 2 & 4 Section working on construction of HILLS CAMP at A2d.75. composed of NISSEN huts & corrugated iron & pcd structure. CELLAR CAMP at A3a & A3c composed of cellar shelters principally No. 3 Section worked on improvement of shelters & c.a.b. providing same new accommodation at CUBITT CAMP & HANSON CAMP. A2a & A9c. No. 1 Section extended Roff to Ammunition dump at A8C.66. also the Return dump at A8C.66. Infantry parties assisted in all the above work. Plans were made showing all accommodation.	
	28-31		LE PENDU CAMP & WINNIPEG CAMP were improved. MONT ST. ELOY.	
	27-31		An officer of this Cy arrived upon the improvement of three standings & accommodation in the Divisional area assisting same in the carrying out of this suggestion, & acting for the supply of material.	
	21		Major BRIGGS D.S.O. R.E. left for the O/Co Conference at BOULOGNE. Capt. CAISWELL R.E. took over command of company in his absence.	
	29		Maj. BRIGGS left BOULOGNE for England on one months sheet leave.	
	30-31		12 Saddles from Load 4747 & 4750. 20 Collar Line Catalor bottles Cr for work done to large armoured trucks in hand.	

1875 Wt. W.593/326 1,000,000 4/15. J.B.C.&A. A.D.S.S./Forms/C. 2118.

WAR DIARY or INTELLIGENCE SUMMARY

Army Form C. 2118

Vol 29 Ord 3

EXTRACT FROM WEEKLY STATES

Date	STRENGTH OFF	STRENGTH OR	REINFORCEMENTS OFF	REINFORCEMENTS OR	TRANSFERS FROM	TRANSFERS TO	KILLED OFF	KILLED OR	CAS FROM	CAS TO	WOUNDED OFF	WOUNDED OR
1917 6 Oct	6	196	-	1	-	-	-	1	-	-	-	3
13 "	6	197	-	5	-	-	-	-	-	1	1 R	3
20 "	6	197	-	1	-	-	-	-	-	1	-	1
27 "	6	201	-	5	-	-	-	-	1	2	1	1
						† evacuation PB	-	1	-	-		

H Muirell
Captain R.E.
for OC 477 S.M. Field Co.

CONFIDENTIAL

War Diary.
of
477 S.M. Field Company. R.E.

Vol 30

(Volume 30)
(Sheets 2)

www.ingramcontent.com/pod-product-compliance
Lightning Source LLC
Chambersburg PA
CBHW081531160426
43191CB00011B/1738